TWAYNE'S WORLD AUTHORS SERIES

A Survey of the World's Literature

SPAIN

Janet W. Diaz, Texas Tech University

EDITOR

Antonio García Gutiérrez

TWAS 565

Antonio García Gutiérrez in 1836

ANTONIO GARCÍA GUTIÉRREZ

By CARMEN IRANZO

TWAYNE PUBLISHERS
A DIVISION OF G. K. HALL & CO., BOSTON

Copyright © 1980 by G. K. Hall & Co.

Published in 1980 by Twayne Publishers,
A Division of G. K. Hall & Co.
All Rights Reserved

Printed on permanent/durable acid-free paper and bound
in the United States of America

First Printing

Library of Congress Cataloging in Publication Data

Iranzo, Carmen.
Antonio García Gutiérrez.

(Twayne's world authors series ; TWAS 565 : Spain)
Bibliography: p. 165–67
Includes index.
1. García Gutiérrez, Antonio, 1813–1884—
Criticism and interpretation.
PQ6523.G2835Z7   862'.5   79-22765
ISBN 0-8057-6407-0

To the Memory of my Father
and Giuseppe Verdi

Contents

Preface
Chronology
1. Life and Works — 15
2. The First Play: *El trovador* — 29
3. The Theater of García Gutiérrez — 44
4. The Decade 1840–1850 — 58
5. Plays from 1850 to 1870 — 92
6. The Last Plays — 112
7. *Zarzuelas* — 128
8. Spain and Giuseppe Verdi — 139
9. Poetry — 145
10. Conclusion — 157
    Notes and References — 161
    Selected Bibliography — 165
    Index — 168

About the Author

Carmen Iranzo Campos was born in the city of Valencia, Spain. After enduring eight years of post-civil war Spain she and her family joined her father, living in exile in Mexico. There she met and married Alva V. Ebersole. After he completed his studies the couple returned to his native USA. She has taught Spanish at Amherst College, the U. of Massachusetts, Adelphi U. and Hofstra University, where she studied and received her M.A. degree in 1968. She lives in Chapel Hill, North Carolina, where her husband is a professor of Spanish literature.

She has done considerable research in Spanish vocal music, from the XIII century Cantigas of Alfonso el Sabio to tonadillas of the XVIII century, as well as in Golden Age Spanish theater. She has performed as an actress and singer since adolescence, and has appeared as soloist and concert artist in more than a hundred different occasions, including performances with the Long Island Choral Society, the Adelphi University Opera Workshop and the Hollywood Wilshire Symphony Association, among others. With her husband she has helped produce and has appeared in more than fifteen Spanish plays in New York, Chapel Hill, and El Paso, Texas, where recently she received an award for her costumes at the Siglo de Oro Festival.

She has published articles and book reviews in *Hispanófila*, read scholarly papers at meetings of the Modern Language Association, American Association of Teachers of Spanish and Portuguese, the Asociación Internacional de Hispanistas, Moutain Interstate Foreign Language Conference, and others. She has also published short stories in several publications, including *Insula, Voces de Mañana* (Harper and Row), *Cinco Cuentistas Contemporáneos,* (Prentice Hall) and the following books: Roberto de Nola's *Libro de cozina,* (Taurus, Madrid, 1969), which is the first cookbook printed in Castillian, translated in 1525 from the Catalan edition of 1520; an edition of *Los Amantes de Teruel* by Andrés Rey de Artieda and Tirso de Molina (Taurus, Madrid, 1971); *Agridulce,* a collection of original short stories, (Mediterráneo, Madrid, 1974); an edition of *La niñaa de Gómez Arias* by Luis Vélez de Guevara and Pedro Calderon de la Barca, in Colección Siglo de Oro, (Valencia, 1974); an edition of Linton Lomas Barret's study of *Como padre y como rey,* by Juan Pérez de Montalbán, (Estudios de Hispanófila, No. 39, Madrid, 1976), and a book in this series, No. 501, *Juan Eugenio Hartzenbusch* (Boston, 1978). She is currently working on a critical edition of Hartzenbusch's *Los Amantes de Teruel* for Ediciones Cátedra; Madrid.

Preface

Antonio García Gutiérrez occupies an enviable place in Spanish Romanticism. Of the many names that come to mind when one mentions that period, his is one that could stand alone on the merits of a single play: *El trovador* (The Troubadour). This title is lure enough to read or study more of his production; if the fame of this play is due in great part to the popularity of the opera bearing that title, by Giuseppe Verdi, this honor is not only well deserved, but it is shared with many other titles produced by other authors of the same period. The matter will be discussed further in a chapter dealing with García Gutiérrez and the relationship of Romanticism with him and the operas of Verdi.

A man known among his contemporaries for his unassuming air, lyric vein, and an all-around goodness that seemed linked to his poetic inspiration, García Gutiérrez enriched Spanish theater in a consistent way, with more successful plays than failures, and these so classified mainly in contrast with his best. Taking as his plots Spanish themes, historic figures, legends, or anchoring his tale here and there in real happenings, people or places, his portrayals and situations have an unusual ability to bring to the surface varying emotions, depicted with a vocabulary rich in beauty. His poetry possesses a similar quality, and a freshness that gives the impression that the author is living it. Some of his sketchy or incomplete poems seem to be more an experiment than a composition; at times they contain ideas later developed into a play, or his notes and thoughts on a legend or episode to be treated dramatically.

Of lesser importance are his librettos for *zarzuelas*, although these two branches of endeavor, poetry and librettos, seem to have been relegated to second place in favor of the theater. His travels and residence abroad seem to have had little effect on his artistic efforts other than his assimilating or exploring things that caught his fancy, and this probably can be said only of his stay in Havana and Mérida, his first venture abroad. His diplomatic posts later kept him away from his country, but his talent was not geared to any particular place other than his own mind and the rich history and legends of Spain. Therefore García Gutiérrez's impact is purely artistic, and although no one can do justice to his beautiful language in translation, I hope to convey something of the quality that makes this dramatist and poet appreciated in his native Spain.

I have deliberately omitted some works and opinions of authors and scholars whose absence will be noticed by Hispanists, for the reason that they do not add substantially to earlier studies by contributing more material, or because they contain errors. In the absence of an edition of the complete works of García Gutiérrez, those collections now existing will be commented upon. More importance is given to individual plays, in chronological order, since our author's production is rather large. Biographical information concerning Antonio García Gutiérrez is very scarce, therefore little more can be added to what is generally known.

CARMEN IRANZO

Chronology

1813 Born in Chiclana, Cádiz, July 5.
1833 Went to Madrid with a friend, on foot.
1834 Began to translate Scribe plays.
1835 Wrote his most famous play, *El trovador* (The Troubadour), and joined the army.
1836 *El trovador* presented.
1837 Presented *El page* (The Page Boy) in May; composition of *El rey monge* (The Monk King), based on a historical figure.
1840 Published a book of his poems; *El Encubierto de Valencia* (The Disguised Man of Valencia) is performed in July.
1841 Performance of *El caballero de industria* (The Cunning Gentleman), a humorous play supposedly written before going to Madrid.
1842 *Luz y tinieblas* (Light and Darkness), poetry, is published.
1843 Presented *Simón Bocanegra*.
1844 García Gutiérrez left for the Americas: Mérida (México) and Cuba. Wrote several plays and translated some from the French.
1846 Wrote *Los hijos del tío Tronera* (Uncle Tronera's Children), a parody of *El trovador*, performed in 1849.
1850 Returns to Spain; Giuseppe Verdi sets *El trovador* to music, performed in 1851 as *Il trovatore*.
1853 First zarzuela: *La espada de Bernardo* (Bernard's Sword). Second and most popular *zarzuela: El grumete* (The Shipboy).
1855 Travels to London with a government post. Many writings lost in a fire in his brother's house.
1856 Awarded the medal of King Carlos III.
1857 Giuseppe Verdi sets *Simón Bocanegra* to music.
1858 García Gutiérrez returns to Spain.
1862 Becomes member of the Royal Spanish Academy.
1863 *La vuelta del corsario* (The Return of the Pirate), a sequel to *El grumete*, is performed in November.
1864 Receives several honors and medals. *Venganza catalana*

(Catalan Revenge) presented; the author was crowned on stage.
1865 Presentation of *Juan Lorenzo*, the play that most satisfied García Gutiérrez.
1865 *El capitán negrero* (The Slave-dealer Captain), his last *zarzuela*.
1866 A volume of his selected plays is presented to him in homage.
1868 Serves as consul of Spain in Bayonne.
1869 Becomes consul of Spain in Genoa.
1872 Director of the Museum of Archaeology in Madrid.
1880 Last play: *Un grano de arena* (A Grain of Sand).
1884 Dies in Madrid, August 26.

CHAPTER 1

Life and Works

I Biography

ANTONIO García Gutiérrez was born in Chiclana, a village in the province of Cádiz, in southern Spain, July 5, 1813 (some books quote 1812 as the year of his birth). His father wanted him to study medicine, and he was enrolled in the University of Cádiz. The young man, more inclined to poetry, would compose his verses on the sly, and in very small handwriting, to confuse his father and make him believe that they were class notes. This practice damaged his eyesight.

At the age of twenty, with a friend, and with papers that only allowed them to go as far as Pinto, near Madrid, he started for the capital, on foot, a trip lasting seventeen days. By this time young Antonio had already composed a fair number of poems and four plays. He encountered rough times in Madrid as he was unfamiliar with the ways of the city, and it was difficult to enter literary circles, although he finally managed. He sustained himself by working at different publishing houses, more intent on having his own efforts printed than making a living.

Having established a beachhead, as it were, he published a few things, and read other of his writings to his peers; one such effort was *El trovador,* which was not liked by the group that heard it. Discouraged and poor, he enlisted in the army and was stationed at Leganés. A comic actor, Antonio Guzmán, selected the play for a performance in his own honor, although he had no role in it. García Gutiérrez left his army post in uniform to attend the performance. The clamor was such he had to go on stage to receive the applause and enthusiastic reaction of the public, a feat unknown until then in Spanish theaters.[1] This turning point in his life came on March 1, 1836. More plays of uneven quality followed, including the very successful performance of *Simón Bocanegra*. Discouraged by jealousies and unfair treatment suffered from those envious of his talents, in 1844 García Gutiérrez went to Santander, and a month later sailed for Cuba. His stay there was most rewarding, as was that in Mérida, in the península of Yucatán, México. During his stay in the Américas, García Gutiérrez wrote several plays, some original, some translated from the French, a task begun before leaving Spain. He returned to his country in 1850, after some six years' absence.

During his three years with a government post in London, from 1855 to 1858, he received the news of a fire in the house of his brother in Sevilla, where he had stored many of his writings. One of the plays lost was *Roger de Flor,* which he subsequently wrote again from memory as *Venganza catalana* (Catalan Revenge). In the intervening years, between diplomatic duties, he received various academic and artistic distinctions. Upon the death of Antonio Gil de Zárate in 1862, García Gutiérrez was selected to fill the former's chair as a member of the Royal Spanish Academy. Four medals were awarded our author, the first that of King Carlos III, in 1856; in 1864 he received another, that of the Concepción of Villaviciosa, a Portuguese honor; two more followed, the María Victoria medal when first established, and the Cross of Isabel la Católica. In 1866 the only volume of his plays known to date was compiled and presented to him as an homage. Some of his best works are in that collection, including some previously sold, to which he had no copyright. Later, his duties as Consul in Bayonne and Genoa, as well as his other positions, were laced with more plays. At the time of his death in 1884, he was director of the Museum of Archaeology of Madrid, a post he had occupied since 1872.

There seems to be a consensus among the scholars of his time that García Gutiérrez deserved all the distinctions he received. He is depicted as a good, affable man, of vast erudition, conscientious in his work, and considerate of others, traits that made for a winning personality. The beauty he experienced was reflected in his poems and plays—the poet always at work. Depicting feelings in the theater through his inspired works had the doubleeffect of involving the audience not only emotionally, but also with the sheer lyricism of his verses. His artistic achievement was recognized on the occasion of the performance of the acclaimed *Venganza catalana* by a crown of laurel which was placed on him on stage, followed by many others deposited or tossed onto the stage.[2]

What García Gutiérrez wrote, be it for the theater or for reading, is not necessarily mild and happy; in his production there are scenes and situations so powerful and sad that screams or tears would be the more likely reaction. Here is precisely where García Gutiérrez is a master: dramatic emotion reaches tremendous heights, but always with a poetic element that precludes anger in favor of sorrow. As he lived and left his impact in the theater, so was he honored. Although he requested a simple burial, family, friends, and men of letters disregarded his wishes, making his funeral procession their final homage. Accounts of the funeral describe it as a real public tribute; to the profusion of crowns and flowers covering the casket, an actress added a crown of laurel.

As is often the case, there is practically no detailed biographical information about this author. I have not been more successful in finding additional items than others before me, or even in locating many of his works; no collection exists other than the already-mentioned volume of selected plays, and his poems. The name *Antonio*, followed by two surnames as common in Spain as *García* and *Gutiérrez*, makes tracing his family practically impossible. There is passing reference to the wedding of his daughter, his son-in-law being Fernando Navarro, one of those who admired and wished to honor him, and the birth of a granddaughter. This clearly indicates a good family life, but there are no names available to us, either of his wife or any children.

In my futile efforts to find biographical material, I consulted a curious book[3] listing celebrities from different epochs, in which it is stated that contemporary prominent figures are excluded, because only posterity could judge whether they would merit inclusion. A similar publication, unfortunately dealing with other names, enhances the idea of having one's contemporaries do a biography, since in such a case the writer has the unequaled opportunity to see the person, cultivate his friendship, know the man as well as the artist. Both points of view have their merits, but neither has provided any more data on García Gutiérrez.

One trait that seems to distinguish this particular author is the fact that, unless translating a given piece, as he did from the French, his themes are Spanish, although the conflict or part of it may be the fruit of his imagination and not drawn from history. Even when

García Gutiérrez takes a historic character and weaves a story about him, the author seems to stay within the realm of spiritual problems, which surface even when the situation ranges from revenge to politics, from immorality to tyranny. Sentimentality imbues the poet, who follows his inspiration above everything, and cannot deal with even the most distasteful of situations without imparting to them a quality that softens them in some way. According to his contemporary Antonio Ferrer del Río, who writes about him in 1846, García Gutiérrez had a tendency to slow down after a successful play, and had to be coerced to produce another gem. At times laziness apparently crept into his intellect: after an unsatisfactory experience he was inactive for a time, as if unwilling to rectify or learn from his mistakes; then a new flare of activity would come and another beautiful play would be the result.

Cayetano Rosell observes that what came from the pen of García Gutiérrez was always polished, conveying exactly what the author had in mind, as if formed there complete with versification. This appraisal seems to me more plausible than Ferrer del Río's concept. Not all writers work alike; for some the idea has only a nebulous shape and does not become precise until the writing begins. Others elaborate considerably before starting. García Gutiérrez could have had the type of mind that works in the background, maturing the idea without letting even the writer know of its presence, to emerge when it is ready. Then the urge to write becomes so intense that the hand may not be fast enough; the readiness includes the proper vocabulary, because with the idea comes shape, movement, an inner picture the mind has to describe, thus providing the emotions and the words to depict it. In the case of a poet, then, it is not surprising that it may come to him already in verse form.

Since García Gutiérrez did not have to rely on his writings to make a living, as he had no trouble holding good positions, and not being involved in politics or research as time-consuming endeavors, one can conclude he wrote mostly when inspired, when the proper elements were so disposed as to be propitious. Perhaps his lesser efforts were done under pressure or as a commission. In his advanced age, despite the scarcity of biographical material, his mind appears to have been not clear at times, but suddenly a spark would produce another good play. This can be deduced from the illness that eventually took his life, as he died of a cerebral hemorrhage.

II Antonio García Gutiérrez and Romanticism

The Romantic period, that revolutionary movement which changed all literature in a renewal process not lacking in imitations, crossing borders with the sole purpose of artistic interchange, was enhanced and reaffirmed in Spain by the first performance of Antonio García Gutiérrez's *El trovador*. The circumstances surrounding such a happening have been called strange by more than one scholar, and indeed they were. The young author had gone to Madrid in search of wider horizons for his literary talents, but success had not accompanied him; so, discouraged, he had joined the army as a means of survival. Catapulted to fame so suddenly by the first performance of *El trovador* García Gutiérrez found himself in a difficult position, due to his total unpreparedness to pursue an avenue open to him that he could not refuse to take. The first landmark had already been made in the Romantic theater in Spain by Angel de Saavedra, later Duque de Rivas, and his *Don Alvaro o la fuerza del sino* (Don Alvaro or the Power of Fate). Saavedra had been in exile in Paris along with Francisco Martínez de la Rosa and others. The latter had already published *La conjuración de Venecia* (The Conspiracy at Venice) in the capital of France in 1830; it was first performed in Cádiz in 1832, and not in Madrid until 1834.

Whatever influence these dramatists may have received in France, and no book can be consulted that does not credit Victor Hugo and Alexander Dumas in that aspect, the Spaniards used such influence in their own way, taking only what could serve their purpose and not copying blindly. The interesting point in this connection is that Victor Hugo had in turn drawn from his childhood stay in Spain memories and elements that had impressed him,[4] making no secret of this source, although many of his fellow Frenchmen prefer to ignore. More than one type can be traced easily from his own account of his stay in Spain. His *Hernani*, a landmark in the Romantic period, exemplifies inspiration in reverse, since if Hugo had an impact on the Spanish exiles, the Spaniards had left an earlier mark on him.

Polemics to the contrary notwithstanding, examination of literary history makes clear that the Romantic movement was not merely copied in Spain, but was rather a return to habits and dissensions from norms in theater productions that other countries defended;

the authors of the seventeenth and eighteenth centuries in Spain had been doing for many years what the Romantics advocated as if by common agreement. The same scholars that find an influence of Dumas or Hugo, naming a specific play as the source for some of the Spanish works, come to the conclusion that there were already antecedents in the production of Calderón de la Barca and others of his contemporaries. The Spanish Classic authors, in turn, had found their inspiration often in historical episodes, so that the Romantics were not so much copying contemporaries as retelling an old story in a new language.

The originality of *Don Alvaro o la fuerza del sino* has been discussed and proven; what makes it more appealing are precisely the historical episodes and places from which the author took a little, just enough to make his story ring true. Angel de Saavedra was returning from exile, from the one place where he could have been influenced, while Antonio García Gutiérrez, who had not yet set foot outside Spain, was less likely to be an imitator. Unlike some of his contemporaries, such as Juan Eugenio Hartzenbusch, born in Madrid and attracted to the theater from an early age, the Duque de Rivas or (older) Martínez de la Rosa, immersed in politics, young Antonio García Gutiérrez arrived in Madrid seeking to do that which he could not accomplish in his native Chiclana. With a set of experiences different from those born in Madrid, our author frequented the Parnasillo, a dark and dirty café next to the Príncipe Theater (immortalized by Larra) where aspiring poets, artists of all kinds, journalists, and politicians gathered. The main fare being conversation rather than consumption of refreshments, since most of them were very poor, the Parnasillo was a proving ground for poets and writers to air and test their efforts, with mixed reactions on the part of critics and listeners. There García Gutiérrez tried out some of his poetry, as well as parts of his plays, including *El trovador*.

Guillaume Huszar, in his studies of comparative literature, explores Spanish influence on the French theater of the eighteenth and nineteenth centuries (as he had done before with the seventeenth). Aside from obvious traits and translations, Huszar observes that Corneille was fascinated by the *hidalgos* (Spanish gentlemen) as an ideal he could not attain, and for that reason the *comedia* was so important to him. Lesage possessed a mischievous spirit and all he had to do was to read the picaresque to fire his talent. This type of influence is what Huszar terms the Spanish *genius,* explained further with the comment that copying a few lines or a passage from a play does not mean that someone's work is "influenced," because they lack the essential spirit. The literature of each country is formed by its own laws, taking from the foreign writings that which suits the national character, or *genius*. In the case of England and Spain, physically isolated from the rest of Europe, that separation accounts for the originality of their respective theaters. In the Spanish *comedia*, Huszar continues, the genres appear mixed, because from the reaction of the characters springs the freedom of form. This characteristic continues and surfaces with Romanticism. Victor Hugo was permeated with things Spanish, and his genius is chivalrous. The chivalrous spirit Huszar mentions is the sum of the worship of God, loyalty to the king (elected by divine providence and therefore the supreme being on earth), and loyalty to the laws of honor and love; in short, everything which medieval poetry had sanctified. Huszar is of the opinion that Victor Hugo applied to his own work the same spirit that Lope de Vega and others had, and even if he does not mention Spain often, it was so much a part of him that the defense of freedom in art was only a manifestation of the direct or indirect influence of centuries, which came natural to him. Pride, honor, and other such feelings, stemming from an exaggerated concept of personal worth and dignity, can become instruments by which others are sacrificed. These elements are taken to extremes in the *comedia*, and in this respect Hugo does not fall far behind.

Alexander Weil, in his introduction to his memoirs (Paris, 1890), says that Hugo not only used all the chivalrous traits of the Spaniard, but was a Spanish Catholic at heart, so that in all his works there is a sediment of inquisition, poison, a dagger, and incense. Huszar concludes that Hugo's plots have extreme situations, as in the *comedia*. Some such plays are *Angelo,* after Calderón's *El médico de su honra* (The Surgeon of His Honor); *Marion de Lorme,* after Cervantes's *La tía fingida* (The Feigned Aunt), which also preceeds *Manon; Torquemada,* set in Barcelona; *Lucrèce Borgia* deals with a Spanish family; there is "jesuitism" in *Cromwell,* and the Esmeralda of *Notre Dame de Paris* resembles Cervantes's *La gitanilla* (The Gypsy Girl). *Hernani* and *Le roi s'amuse* will be briefly commented upon in the chapter on Verdi. Other French writers are similarly treated by Huszar, but they are beyond the scope of this book.

Enrique López Funes, in his study of the works of Antonio García

Gutiérrez[5] recognizes the importance of Victor Hugo as a driving force to establish Romanticism, but while the French brand is full of tyrants, assassins, traitors, mysterious crimes, and effectism in the theater, tending more to the physiological aspects of passion than the moral, the Spanish variety draws from chronicles, traditions, tales, popular sayings, and Spanish *comedias*. López Funes considers *Don Alvaro o la fuerza del sino* unsurpassed as a single work, but for him the brightest Romantic dramatist is Antonio García Gutiérrez, to whom he gives credit for shedding elements alien to his true inspiration and being his own strictest censor. He detects in him a revolutionary element which Pérez Galdós called liberal; certain things are no longer just for the upper class, and the sea is now called by its name, not Neptune. Fighting the oppressor, the poor against the rich, vengeance against offense are equalizing forces, but García Gutiérrez does not exalt these ideas; he has enough strength to hurl pathetic drama into the arena of the historic and political. Even when he portrays a despicable character, taken from someone else's fantasy, says López Funes, the author cannot avoid projecting his own beauty by gilding the background and the frame. His spontaneity of inspiration makes him at times follow the action or resolve a situation as it would logically result from what the characters are doing, not in accord with a plot calculated beforehand. This is one reason some of his characters are repeated in part or in whole in later plays. García Gutiérrez leaves a lingering impression as the mark of his genius. As an example, López Funes mentions some plays he considers laden with horrible situations or lacking in verisimilitude, but imbued with such artistry and artistic truth that artistic beauty does not depend on the moral. García Gutiérrez trascends fiction to the point that no actor can do justice to some of his characters. Regrettably, only a few plays are discussed by López Funes in his difficult-to-find book, for which reason many possibly interesting judgments will be found missing (see note 5 of this chapter).

An element imported to Spain by the Bourbon family was Italian music, familiar to many because of the mutual influence exercised by musicians in both countries, since Spanish composers, chapel masters, and preceptors had been in Italy occupying prominent posts for several hundred years. The Mediterranean light, sounds, and characters in general have to be taken into consideration as a common bond. García Gutiérrez was to bring a consistent level of

Life and Works 23

lyricism, emotion, and a quality of immediacy to his verse which by itself could have filled any theater. In his day, his librettos for *zarzuelas* must have been very gratifying, but it is only the musical composer who habitually is given credit. Among the musicians for whom García Gutiérrez prepared texts are some prominent in the field: Emilio Arrieta, Manuel Fernández Caballero, and Francisco Asenjo Barbieri. The latter was the most inclined to imitate the Italians, but even he was unable to shed his very Spanish vein, as any excerpt of his music indicates. García Gutiérrez fits quite differently into the mosaic of Spanish Romanticism and that of the entire Romantic movement, usually omitting references to politics of the day, but not of the historic past, making his work a constant offering of sentimental and lyric beauty.

III *The Author and His Works*

Unfortunately there is no collection of Antonio García Gutiérrez's complete works, so we will have to restrict ourselves to the known anthologies, and will comment on pieces found scattered in old libraries. Booksellers answer with a consistent "no" to inquiries about even some of his most renowned plays. Although the chronology is doubtful, and an attempt will be made to keep the works in that order, the volumes published do not follow it for obvious reasons. First we have *Poesías* (Poems, Madrid: Boix, 1840). A short foreword by the author tells of his printing his poetry at the request of a publisher, not looking for public recognition. On this count he notes that some of the poems included are understood only by him, since they deal with a moment, a remembrance, or some other thing dear to him; this is a concession to his ego. Some, he adds, are not in tune with the taste of the times, being the product of his admiration for Spanish poets of the seventeenth and eighteenth centuries, a fact he does not consider a fault; but, he concludes, he is not the one who should judge them—the critics will take pleasure doing that. The small book, totaling almost 300 pages nevertheless, contains thirty-one compositions of different meters and themes (one called a tale), excerpts of a lyric drama, and a dramatic fantasy in five acts.

Luz y tinieblas (Light and Darkness, Madrid: Boix, 1842) is divided into two parts, with some items missing in the index. The first contains historic *romances* (ballads), with others also found in the second, the first portion of which is dedicated to religious poems. *Obras escogidas de Don Antonio García Gutiérrez* (Selected Works, Madrid: Rivadeneyra, 1866) contains a prologue by Juan Eugenio Hartzenbusch. This collection is conceived as a tribute to the author. It is stated in the prologue that three publishers gave permission to use some of García Gutiérrez's plays, then their property, for *one time only*. Among these were some of the best titles of our author. The queen and several noblemen contributed money for the printing, although others in government were less enthusiastic. Some incomplete biographical data and lavish praise for the honored writer follow. Nineteen plays are included, three of them in an appendix: *El trovador* (The Troubadour), *El page* (The Page Boy), *El rey monge* (The Monk King), *Juan Dándolo, Samuel, El Encubierto de Valencia* (The Disguised Man of Valencia), *Simón Bocanegra, Afectos de odio y amor* (Feelings of Hate and Love), *El tesorero del rey* (The King's Treasurer), *La espada de Bernardo* (Bernard's Sword), *El grumete* (The Ship-boy), *La cacería real* (The Royal Hunt), *La bondad sin la experiencia* (Goodness without Experience), *Un duelo a muerte* (A Duel to the Death), *La vuelta del corsario* (The Return of the Pirate), *Venganza catalana* (Catalan Revenge), *Juan Lorenzo, El capitán negrero* (The Slave-dealer Captain), and *Las cañas se vuelven lanzas* (The Reeds Turn into Spears).

Most other plays by García Gutiérrez are found in Teatro Español and Teatro Español Borrás. Volumes 202, 203, 204, 205, and 206 of the set (numbered as housed in the library at the University of North Carolina, Chapel Hill), as well as some in Borrás, contain them. Other writings by our author comprise speeches for the Spanish American Academy, a historic description of the Archaeological National Museum, and a speech on popular Castilian poetry for an event honoring the poet Manuel José Quintana, 1855. Plays written in cooperation with other writers are: *El sitio de Bilbao* (The Siege of Bilbao), 1837, with Isidoro Gil; *Juan Dándolo*, 1839, with José Zorrilla; *El tejedor de Játiva* (The Weaver from Játiva), 1849, with Eduardo and Eusebio Asquerino; *El tesorero del rey* (The King's Treasurer), 1850, with Eduardo Asquerino; and *La Baltasara*, 1852, with Agustín Príncipe and Antonio Gil de Zárate.

García Gutiérrez's translations are numerous: From Scribe are *El vampiro* (The Vampire), 1834; *Batilde*, 1835; *El cuákero y la cómica* (The Quaker and the Actress), 1836; *La pandilla o la elección de un diputado* (The Gang or the Election of a Representative),

Life and Works

1837; from Alexander Dumas are *Calígula*, 1839; *Don Juan de Mariana o la caída de un ángel* (Don Juan de Mariana or the Fall of an Angel), 1839; and *Margarita de Borgoña*, 1840. Other translations are *El hijo del emigrado* (The Son of the Immigrant), 1843, from A. Bourgeois; *La ópera y el sermón* (The Opera and the Sermon), 1843, by Laurencin; *El galán invisible* (The Invisible Suitor), 1843, from Mellesville; *La gracia de Dios* (The Grace of God, also found as the *Saboyana o la gracia de Dios*), 1846, from Gustave Lemoine; *Un día de reinado* (One Day of Reign), 1854, with D. L. Olona, from Scribe and St. Georges; *Un duelo a muerte* (A Duel to the Death), 1860, an imitation of Lessing's *Emilia Galotti*; *Dos coronas* (Two Crowns), 1861; *El hijo de familia o el lancero voluntario* (The Playboy or the Voluntary Lancer), 1854, with two other authors not identified positively; *Juan de Suavia*, 1841, with Isidoro Gil, all from the French without specifics; billed only as translations without further identification are *Dos a dos* (Two by Two), 1851, and *Estela o el padre y la hija* (Estela or Father and Daughter) 1839.[6]

In the following list of García Gutiérrez's original plays, chronology may be open to question in some instances, as some works were first performed and later printed, others were presented and published almost simultaneously, and some were never performed or at least there are no extant references to that; therefore the earliest date when in doubt will be taken as the closest. The order so established follows:

1836 *El trovador* (The Troubadour).
1837 *El page* (The Page Boy), *El rey monge* (The Monk King), *Magdalena.*
1838 *El bastardo* (The Bastard).
1839 *Samuel.*
1840 *El Encubierto de Valencia* (The Disguised Man of Valencia), *Los desposorios de Inés* (The Wedding of Ines).
1841 *El caballero de industria* (The Cunning Gentleman), *El caballero leal* (The Loyal Gentleman), *Zaida.*
1842 *El premio del vencedor* (The Prize of the Winner).
1843 *Simón Bocanegra, Las bodas de doña Sancha* (The Wedding of Doña Sancha), *De un apuro otro mayor* (From Trouble a Bigger One).
1844 *Gabriel, Los alcaldes de Valladolid* (The Mayors of Valladolid), *Empeños de una venganza* (The Pledges of a Vengeance), *La mujer valerosa* (The Brave Woman).
1845 *El secreto del ahorcado* (The Secret of the Hung Man).
1846 *Los hijos del tío Tronera* (The Children of Uncle Tronera).

1850 *Afectos de odio y amor* (Feelings of Hate and Love).
1851 *Los millonarios* (The Millionaires).
1853 *La espada de Bernardo* (Bernard's Sword), *El grumete* (The Shipboy).
1854 *La cacería real* (Royal Hunt).
1855 *La bondad sin la experiencia* (Goodness without Experience).
1858 *Azón Visconti*.
1859 *El robo de las sabinas* (The Rape of the Sabines), *Cegar para ver* (To Become Blind in Order to See).
1861 *Llamada y tropa* (Call and Troop).
1862 *Galán de noche* (Night Suitor), *La tabernera de Londres* (The Tavern Keeper Girl of London).
1863 *La vuelta del corsario* (The Return of the Pirate), *Eclipse parcial* (Partial Eclipse).
1864 *Venganza catalana* (Catalan Revenge), *Las cañas se vuelven lanzas* (The Reeds Turn into Spears).
1865 *Juan Lorenzo, El capitán Negrero* (The Slave-dealer Captain).
1871 *Sendas opuestas* (Opposite Paths).
1872 *Nobleza obliga* (Nobility Obliges), *Doña Urraca de Castilla* (Doña Urraca of Castile), *Crisálida y mariposa* (Chrysalis and Butterfly).
1877 *Un cuento de niños* (A Children's Story).
1880 *Un grano de arena* (A Grain of Sand).

Some of these titles are *zarzuelas*, and not all are completely original, but they are included in the section dealing with *zarzuelas* because of the special kind of theater they are. With that exception, all the original titles will be discussed except *Los alcaldes de Valladolid*, which I was unable to locate.

IV About the Collections Consulted

A great many García Gutiérrez plays have the names of the cast printed in the particular edition, pointing to the fact that they were performed, although in some cases there is no information about the first performance. Most plays state whether they are the sole property of the author or of the publisher, meaning that the dramatic company director may have purchased the original play and later sold it to a publisher or a printer. This practice was challenged at various times by the authors in view of the fact that even with very successful plays their creators were not entitled to royalties of any kind, and they were forbidden by law to publish or make other use of their work. Such is the case with some of García Gutiérrez's early

Life and Works

and famous plays. Many issues of his dramatic works contain a statement of ownership, usually a given editor, at times the printer or a bookseller, and after 1852 the author himself, although *La espada de Bernardo,* for instance, dated 1853, is not the property of García Gutiérrez. Such rights are detailed in the cover of *Un grano de arena,* 1880, where the Administración Lírico Dramática provides a list of works with title, number of acts, name of the author, and what amount is owned by the publisher as specified by the words *half* or *all.* In the case of *Un grano de arena* it is half. For *zarzuelas* title, acts, and composer or author (not both in some cases), are listed with the initials L and M, meaning words and music, and indicating the rights (1/2, for instance, means exactly that).

The back cover of the 1852 edition of *El caballero de industria* proclaims it the property of the director of the Biblioteca Dramática, Vicente Lalama, since he bought the rights from Ignacio Boix, publisher of Ediciones Teatro Moderno Español; some issues bear the note of the previous ownership. The inside cover of *Un cuento de niños,* 1877, lists plays, number of acts, and name of the author, with the proportion the Administración Lírico Dramática owns; in most cases it is all. The back inside cover has a similar listing for *zarzuelas,* with the code for words and music. The Administración Lírico Dramática has power to give permission for performance and collect the appropriate fees. A similar note in *Llamada y tropa,* a *zarzuela,* concerns the distributor, Galería Dramática El Teatro. All these notices point to successive reforms in the laws pertaining to authors' rights and contracts or agreements made among publishers, distributors, and authors.[7] Another curious item appears on the last page of *El tesorero del rey:* a tariff or rate to be charged theaters for the right to perform a play, according to its category which is also listed. Specific theater houses were considered first class in Barcelona, Cádiz, Sevilla, and Valencia, in alphabetical order; some were second class in Cádiz, Granada, Málaga, Palma, and Valladolid. Those in third class are found in many cities as well as fairly large towns, while fourth class comprises primarily theaters within organizations of some kind, regardless of location. Madrid theaters are not listed in any way. The tariff is set according to such things as number of acts, whether it is a first performance, original or not, with a uniform rate for *zarzuelas.* A note states there are rates available according to duration of rental of the locale, by night, week, or season. These and other curious items are helpful in shaping a picture of the theater of the times, since information of that type is not found in critical editions of plays. The practical side brings us to the real world of the authors and those who take part in the production of plays and their dissemination in print.

CHAPTER 2

The First Play: El trovador

I El trovador *(The Troubadour)*

A drama in five acts, in verse and prose, *El trovador* was first performed in the Príncipe Theater, March 1, 1836. The earliest version consulted, in *Obras escogidas*, bears no date or the name of the publisher (it was not the property of the author, and the first publisher gave permission only for it to be reproduced once). The drama takes place in Aragon, during the fifteenth century.

Act one, "The Duel," begins in the palace of the Aljafería, in Zaragoza, as Jimeno tells Ferrando and Guzmán (two other servants of Nuño de Artal, Count of Luna), the story of the Count's brother, who became very sick after a gypsy cast a spell upon him; his nurse reported having seen witches playing ball with the child. The gypsy was caught and burned at the stake. The child improved but soon disappeared. Later his charred body was found where the gypsy had been burned, and everyone suspected her daughter had done it. The spirit of the old woman comes back from time to time as a crow or as a nightowl. Guzmán then recounts the present troubles of the Count of Luna, who loves Leonor de Sesé, while she prefers a troubadour who comes to serenade her. The Count tried forcefully to enter her room in the palace, but the voice of the troubadour was heard and he went to the garden, suspecting Leonor was there. She first mistook the Count for her lover in the dark night, but the moon shone on his face and she rejected him. Manrique, the troubadour, fought with the Count and wounded him.

The servants hear their master awakening inside and leave to join him. The preceding scene was in prose; the next, in Leonor's room, is in verse. Guillén de Sesé scolds his sister Leonor for not paying attention to the Count of Luna: either she must marry him or enter

29

a convent. When he leaves, Leonor tells Jimena, her maid, of her love for Manrique, who believes she betrayed him the night before. He arrives proclaiming his suspicion but, convinced of her love, he reiterates his own for her, and speaks of the danger he is in as an ally of the Count of Urgel, enemy of Luna. Count Nuño enters and finds Manrique there; they exchange harsh words and exit to fight a duel.

Act two, "The Convent," takes place a year later. In Nuño's chambers, he and Guillén exchange views on the Count of Urgel and how the rebels went to the extreme of killing an archbishop, for which Nuño swears revenge. Guillén asks about his wound of a year ago, but Nuño, sullen, inquires about Guillén's sister. Leonor is about to enter a convent since she refuses to consider the Count as her husband, and because news of the death of the troubadour has reached her. When Guillén leaves, Nuño plots with servants to abduct Leonor. Lope brings news of further sedition, and reveals the rebels are coming, with Manrique (previously presumed dead) at their head.

Scene six shows the locutory, cloister, and church of a convent, where Jimena tries to dissuade Leonor from her plans: the lady says that, with Manrique dead, the convent will give her a shield of protection. However, Leonor knows she will offend God by professing as a nun while still thinking of a man. The women enter the convent, as Ruiz comes with Manrique, who hopes to carry Leonor away before she takes the veil, although he is not sure he should take her from God. As he approaches the locutory a choir of nuns is heard (continuing till the end of the act) while on the other side Ferrando and Guzmán witness the scene of Leonor taking her vows inside. As the novice and nuns come out, passing near Manrique, he lifts his visor and Leonor faints when she recognizes him. Ferrando and Guzmán also realize it is Manrique and leave, while more nuns are seen inside with burning candles.

Act three, "The Gypsy," opens in a hut in the mountains of Biscay. Azucena, a gypsy, sings a sad song and then tells Manrique about her mother's having been burned at the stake for bewitching the Count's son; she built her hut in that very place. She witnessed the terrible sight and avenged her mother days later, building a fire and obeying her voice that clamored for revenge, although she was reluctant to burn the little Count. Entranced and crying, she grabbed the boy and threw him into the flames, only to realize that

The First Play

she had killed her own child. Manrique suspects something, but she assures him he is her son and must avenge her mother. He yearns to have a name, and to make a better life for Azucena. Ruiz comes and the two men leave, as the gypsy muses that she almost gave away her secret. She considers the other child as her son.

The next scene takes place in a cell in the convent of Jerusalem, where Leonor bemoans her fate and asks God's forgiveness for her insincere vows. The voice and lute of the troubadour are heard, to her painful surprise. He appears and in a very powerful scene she is torn between her love for Manrique and her desire not to offend God further by breaking her vows in order to follow the troubadour, while Manrique insists that her vows to him have been broken, and she should not keep a promise made to God under such stress. Leonor faints; Ruiz and a soldier observe that the forces of the king are around, as if they knew of Manrique's presence. The noise of fighting is heard as Leonor recovers, and bells toll as a sign of alarm. Manrique and Leonor leave the convent, but are stopped by Nuño, Guillén, and their soldiers. The bells continue tolling until the end of the act, while the men fight.

Act four, "The Revelation," opens in the army camp; Count Nuño and Guillén prepare to look for Leonor and Manrique, who fled during the struggle. A gypsy is brought in, protesting she is looking for her son. Nuño identifies himself as the Count of Luna and she is visibly surprised; the Count tells the soldiers to free her, but Jimeno recognizes Azucena. Then Nuño orders that she be kept prisoner, but out of his sight. She calls for her son Manrique and the Count thereby learns the troubadour is her son, constituting a double motive for revenge.

In scene four Leonor, torn between her love and her religious vows, is with Manrique in a castle in Castellar. He awakens and tells how, haunted by the story Azucena told him, he had a dream in which, amid a terrible storm, a specter demanding revenge came to him; when he turned to look at Leonor she was a skeleton. He now fears for her safety. Ruiz warns that the Count's men are near, and says a gypsy was apprehended. Manrique tells Leonor that the gypsy is his mother and he must aid her. Leonor, sure that he will die in the attempt to rescue Azucena, asks to go with him, but he refuses.

Act five, "The Execution," unfolds in the palace of the Aljaferia, which has a tower with a grilled window where prisoners are kept.

Leonor arrives accompanied by Ruiz, who leaves her by the outside wall. In a monologue she wonders how she can free Manrique; a voice is heard pleading for the soul of a man about to die; then comes the sound of a lute and Manrique's voice singing that he dies for the love of Leonor, who reacts to his voice and words. The scene alternates among the prayer, Manrique's song, and Leonor's anguish, as she and her lover cannot communicate. She drinks the contents of a flask Ruiz gave her, swearing that the Count will never have her. In scene three Nuño and Guillén, in the Count of Luna's chambers, prepare for the execution of Manrique. The Count thinks maybe a priest should be summoned, but Guillén dissuades him; even the king should not be notified, since he is in Valencia. Leonor is missing, and Nuño realizes he is taking revenge on the troubadour because she rejects his love; he plans that the gypsy will die also, for the murder of his brother. Leonor comes to offer herself in exchange for Manrique's freedom. Nuño first rejects her offer because she is crying for the prisoner, and he wants her to suffer, but ultimately agrees, with the condition that Manrique not go back to Aragon.

The sixth scene shows a dungeon where Azucena and Manrique await their fate; she relates again in detail her mother's burning, and falls asleep. Leonor enters and tells Manrique about having gained his freedom; he reacts violently, thinking of the price she probably paid. She then reveals that she poisoned herself, and Manrique refuses to leave. A light is seen, announcing the arrival of those coming to get Manrique: Leonor dies in his arms, and he tries to sing to her once more. Soldiers enter with Nuño and Guillén, and, upon seeing Leonor dead, lead the troubadour away as Azucena awakens. She asks where her son is, and the Count of Luna forces her to witness his execution from the window. The gypsy tries to stop it, but the signal is given, and lights are taken to the scaffold so Azucena will see her son dead. The gypsy then tells the Count that Manrique was his brother. As Nuño throws her to the ground, swearing, she shouts to her mother that she is avenged, and expires.

Prose is used when the characters are not highborn (servants or the gypsy), even when only one servant is in the scene, as in the conspiracy to abduct Leonor. The language fits each person according to his station in life, and the conflicts or problems he faces. The lyricism of Leonor and Manrique flows in an endless harmonious mixture of beauty, emotion, and anguish, leaving no doubt as to their feelings for each other and the dangers they know surround them and their souls. García Gutiérrez, only twenty-two at the time, already possessed the ability to combine the right artistic resources to convey the precise meaning and achieve the desired effect. He proved so adept at providing the background for his tormented protagonists that a simple stage direction gave the full measure of what was required, although at times no direction was necessary, since the dialogue dictated it. This blend was not, obviously, a product of training, but of his feeling every word and every emotion, and being able to reflect this feeling on stage as well as with words.

II *Mariano José de Larra and* El trovador

All accounts of the first performance of the play begin with a brief description of the young author, his disheartening attempts to produce his play, read in part or in whole and rejected by various theater directors as well as friends, and his decision to join the army to make a living; how the comic actor Antonio Guzmán, who did not have a role in this drama, chose it for his own benefit performance, and the smashing success it was. Antonio García Gutiérrez, absent without leave from his quarters, was forced to go on stage and receive the applause of the enthusiastic audience and had to be lent a jacket for the occasion, since he was wearing his uniform as the low-ranking soldier he was. Word-of-mouth publicity was then the best advertisement to ensure the play's being performed many more times. In addition, there was the review published by Mariano José de Larra on two consecutive days (and issues) in the newspaper *El Español* on March 4 and 5 of 1836. Larra set the tone of his entire review with the statement that *El trovador* belongs to the best school, that of genius, whose only teacher is inspiration, ruled only by feeling and truth.

In his exuberance Larra praised the novice author, marveling at his not having distinguished himself up to then in either politics or letters. Larra's rave review the first day dealt exclusively with the plot, which he clearly remembered very well. The second was dedicated to extolling the beauties and defects of the play. The action kept increasing the interest of the audience to the very end, and Larra compared García Gutiérrez to Shakespeare and Calderón; similar to the Englishman were our author's dramatic resources, while the well-defined natural passions, with the richness and chivalrous characters, were seen as resembling those of the Spaniard. Larra observed that the dominant force was not love, but revenge, constituting two main themes opposed at times, but so intertwined that they could not function separately. There were actually three main characters, although the title suggests that everything hinges upon just one. The Count and Leonor are equally important as the dramatic action develops. Leonor is torn by love, turns to God, and then perjures herself, to die for the man she loves. The gypsy burns her own son by mistake, and keeps the Count's brother, taking revenge in a most horrible way. Manrique, torn by his passion for Leonor, loyalty to his political cause, and the love for the woman who raised him as his mother, whose life he must save, is victimized more than any of the other characters.

Larra found too many things going on at once on stage, but the magnetism of the play and its tremendous force led him to defend its defects on the grounds that it was the first dramatic effort of its author, far superior to many "firsts." He believed the work to be conceived more as a novel, a very good one, but, constrained to the limitations of live action, the material was larger than the mold it had to fill. Larra attributed this excess of wealth of emotions to a certain lack of maturity in the development of the characters; also he noted that comings and goings took place without sufficient motive. He pondered, for instance, whether the Count of Luna was not suspicious of Leonor's sudden change of heart and why he let her visit Manrique; also he found unrealistic the latter's access to the lady's chambers, even in the convent, a feat next to impossible in any period. The critic did not advocate obeying so-called dramatic rules, but asked that what was presented on stage be believable. The inexperience of the new dramatist was blamed for the long dialogues, more lyric than necessary, given the circumstances. Larra praised many of the scenes as having unsurpassed beauty that showed skillful knowledge of dramatic effects.

Partial to the sound of recited verse, Larra advocated this way of writing for the theater because the dramatist can rely on the rhyme, whereas he has to invent a prose that will be pleasing to the ear, an effect more difficult to achieve in a play written in both verse and prose, as this work was. However, in no way did he say he was displeased by such a mixture. After reiterating that the defects enumerated were nothing compared to the beauties found

The First Play

in the play, Larra evaluated the production and performance as such. His first biting remark was that the principal actor always got the leading role, whether suitable for him or not (in this case it was not); the same criterion was applied to the leading actress; yet from the aesthetic point of view, the gypsy and Leonor should have been performed by the suitable actress and not by rank. This was also true of the roles of the troubadour and the Count of Luna. Larra also criticized the personal appearance of one of the actors and remarked about the actresses. Larra closed his review by expressing his approval of the audience's forcing the author to come up onstage to receive an ovation, which Antonio García Gutiérrez did humbly.

The brilliance of Larra, his extremely biting and direct style, and his skill at reflecting his observations made an ever greater impact when barely a year after his review of the *Trovador* he commited suicide. His every word was reread and his judgments reviewed by friends and foes alike.[1] In the case of García Gutiérrez he was constructive, since there was little to fault in this play of the young aspiring writer. García Gutiérrez demonstrated having learned a lesson by revising his masterpiece, modifying things he evidently had not noticed until the critic scrutinized his play.

The 1851 edition, reworked expressly for the Teatro Español, is all in verse, and contains some changes: the first scene of the first act takes place in the same palace of Aljaferia, but outside Leonor's quarters. Ferrando is substituted here for Ortiz, in the service of Leonor. When she awakens, the servants leave and the scene with Jimena and Guillén de Sesé takes place, followed by the arrival of Nuño and the subsequent duel with Manrique. The second act occurs in the convent setting, with the Count of Luna coming out of the church to converse with Guillén about the death of the archbishop and to hear news of Leonor's preparing to become a nun. The scheme to abduct her, to be carried out by Guzmán and Ferrando, and the arrival of Lope with the news of the band of rebels headed by Manrique, lead to the ceremony when Leonor takes the veil.

The third act is in two parts, the first in the hut of the gypsy, who hides in the woods upon hearing the soldiers, who apprehend her after she has told the story of her mother to Manrique and he has left to rescue Leonor. The second part is set in the garden of the convent, not in Leonor's cell. Ruiz and Manrique come over the wall. The fourth act unfolds in Castellar, where Manrique has taken Leonor. Guillén, brought in a prisoner, informs his sister that the troubadour is the son of a gypsy, who is imprisoned. After harsh words between the two men, Manrique does not hesitate to free Guillén in order to try to help Azucena; Leonor is left behind. The fifth act, in two parts, begins in the palace of Aljaferia, where Leonor has gone to try to see the Count of Luna. While she waits, the scene of her anguish with the sound of the voice praying and Manrique singing with his lute takes place. Lope lets her in to see Nuño after the details of the execution have been discussed. The second part takes place in the dungeon. Essentially the changes serve to keep more scenes in one location, with the same scenery. The main plot remains very much the same, with the language changed as necessary when converting prose to verse. The acts do not have an identifying title as did the first version, but their beauty and force have not been lost in the process.

III *The Critics*

In his *Galería de la literatura* (Literary Gallery, Madrid: Mellado, 1846) Antonio Ferrer del Río says of Antonio García Gutiérrez that, although he has some good poems in the second volume, his poetry would not have survived without his other accomplishments. He observes that the women created by García Gutiérrez are sweet and passionate, and the fathers always good.[2] In his opinion, our author produced a gem and then rested for a while, eventually learning from his mistakes. The impact of *El trovador*, however, was so great that, at performances years later, people recited long passages of the play from memory. The beauty and emotion García Gutiérrez so freely gives in his works is, then, his greatest asset.

Juan Eugenio Hartzenbusch in his prologue to García Gutiérrez's *Obras escogidas* (Selected Works, 1866), says the author wrote his *Trovador* imitating *Don Alvaro o la fuerza del sino* (Don Alvaro or the Power of Fate) insofar as he wrote in prose those passages that did not call for verse. He notes that the preceding century was long on rules and short on talent, making predictable the upsurge of Spanish *comedia* with the advent of the Romantics of the caliber of Angel de Saavedra, Antonio García Gutiérrez, and others. Nobody asks anymore what school of writing they follow, says Hartzenbusch; so long as the play is interesting, entertaining and instructive, the label is unimportant. The dramatist is free to take truth and beauty where he finds it and to put it on stage.

Cayetano Rosell, in the book compiled by Pedro de Novo y Colson *Autores dramáticos contemporáneos y joyas del teatro español del siglo XIX* (Contemporary Dramatic Authors and Jewels of the XIX Century Spanish Theater, 1881), considers that in García Gutiérrez the most celebrated element of his Romanticism was an originality that distinguished his from the Germanic or French, as well as from the systematic lyric expression of the Spanish Golden Age theater. Rosell adds that when Larra analyzed *El trovador* and found fault in it, he was only defending an art he had proscribed. García Gutiérrez did not draw from history, but wrought living legends imbued with the spirit of certain social classes from past centuries, staging each episode with such artistry, with the opportune, clear, and lyric language, and with so many more touches of beauty that he ensured the reality of a revolution.

Rosell dedicates many lines to extolling the beauty of expression in García Gutiérrez, attempting to justify his praise so as not to seem flattering, but merely truthful. The gentleness, the natural flow of language and ideas, adaptable to the sublime as well as to his comic characters, are an artistic privilege, since in prose they would be just as appropriate and exact, because García Gutiérrez's ideas flow from his mind already finished, polished, specific, and in verse, because that is the way they are formed within him. Extending the praise of the artist to that of the man, Rosell insists he is not being a flatterer: man must learn from living models, and García Gutiérrez is such a good one. Avoiding a realism that appeals to primitive passions, Rosell says, the author depicted love in its pure form, and if at times a despicable character stains the stage of García Gutiérrez's theater it is only to sink him further into the abyss of his own expiation. That is how Antonio García Gutiérrez felt and thought.

Carlos Guaza, in his *Músicos, poetas y actores* (Musicians, Poets and Actors, 1884), also extols the beauties of García Gutiérrez's theater, particularly the just measure in depicting emotions, with no need to cover mistakes with florid verses; looking to history, legends, and Spanish characteristics for his plays, says Guaza, García Gutiérrez bends to no one set of rules or influences, being entirely Romantic but without leading his protagonists into extreme situations. Concerning the *Trovador,* Guaza says Manrique is interesting in three ways, because of his filial love, his love for Leonor which outweighs everything, and his dedication to a civil cause. His misfortunes are created by the gypsy in her planned revenge, and the jealousy of a rejected suitor of Leonor. The dramatic situations on stage are so forceful that the spectator is moved to heights of emotion by which he is completely overwhelmed; there is a feeling, an art, and something like a force which run through all the characters, compared by the critic to the spirit of God floating over primeval waters.

In his prologue to *La literatura española en el siglo XIX* (The Spanish Literature in the Nineteenth Century, 1891), Father Francisco Blanco García states that the glories of Spanish literature are not well studied abroad because Spain is apathetic and pays no heed to the example of Germany, France, and England. The biographical data on García Gutiérrez are taken from the *Obras escogidas* and so include nothing new. Fr. Blanco García says of *El trovador* (p. 226) that it is different from *Don Alvaro* in that Manrique is not pursued by the former's fatalism; the near proclamation of free love (implicit in the union of Manrique and Leonor) must be searched for not so much in the Aragonese court of the fifteenth century, but in the court of the Count of Poitiers; the ladies and gentlemen of Lope and Calderón did not quite reach such extremes. Observing that fidelity to historic fact is not García Gutiérrez's strong point, Fr. Blanco refers to the marvelous intuition of a great artist which our author possessed. With the bad taste that was the rage of the times, García Gutiérrez, in his opinion, can be situated between Victor Hugo and Alexander Dumas, hence what Fr. Blanco sees as the lack of morals in the impure loves of *El page, Magdalena, El rey monge,* and *El Encubierto de Valencia.* A horrible moral void, a systematic falsification, and a violent imbalance are hidden under the rich veil carved by the author with the treasures lent him by his poetic language.

Enrique López Funes finds *El trovador* an extraordinary piece in every respect, although some scenes are hard to believe, especially in the case of Guillén de Sesé and the Count of Luna, but they are less well defined characters than the "stars," the gypsy, Manrique, and Leonor. López Funes detects a French influence in the form and some situations, which García Gutiérrez shed later on, but opines that at the first try he equaled Shakespeare and his *Romeo and Juliet.*

In his book on the Romantic plays of García Gutiérrez (1922), Nicholson Adams gives résumés of plots, not always accurate in important scenes, and adds his vision and evaluation. More interested in finding influences than in the plays themselves, Adams treads dangerous territory when seeking the origins of *El trovador.* When citing Larra's *Macías,* which he says is taken from Lope's *Porfiar hasta morir* (To Struggle until Death), Adams overlooks more relevant material at his disposal, such as the *Cancionero de Baena* and other sources I mention elsewhere,[3] favoring the thesis of Rennert and Regensburger. He points out that by creating the gypsy, García Gutiérrez introduced the element of revenge into a story of ill-fated love and cites, among other characters seeking revenge, Victor Hugo's *Marie Tudor,* Dumas's *Catherine Howard,* and Leonor's brothers in *Don Alvaro o la fuerza del sino.* While the first two titles deal with historic figures who had reason to strike back, the Spanish play he mentions is fictitious.

Adams ventures that García Gutiérrez must have been accustomed to seeing gypsies in his native Andalucía, and to hearing tales of abducted children, such as in *La Gitanilla* and *Notre Dame de Paris.* Assuming García Gutiérrez had indeed read them, there is insufficient basis to conclude he used any of them in any form, since these possible models are by no means the only troubadours, people seeking revenge or gypsies, in real life or in Spanish tradition. Adams notes that while most stolen children were saved by being recognized on time, not so Manrique. The end of *El trovador* therefore reminds him of *Marguerite de Borgogne,* and he adds that fathers, sons, and brothers killing each other without recognition were common happenings in those times. Unfortunately, Adams adduces no evidence to support any of these statements.

Stating that García Gutiérrez copied from the French, labeling each act to give an archaic flavor, Adams fails to see that the author called his play "a drama of chivalry." He wonders whether alternating verse and prose (as Angel de Saavedra had done in his *Don Alvaro o la fuerza del sino*) is not a Shakespearean influence, since it is not a Spanish tradition. Adams contends that Larra did not like the mixture, but I have not found any such statement in Larra's review. Adams likes the play, the way it moves and how it unfolds.

Concerning the intrinsic value of García Gutiérrez, he praises his lyricism, which enhances the worth of his plays and appeals to emotions, not to reason. Making a comparison between the Spanish *comedia* and the Romantic plays, Adams points out that the *comedias* were inherently Romantic, and that their heroes were individuals, not mere types. It is unfortunate that in citing examples, Adams attributes *El tejedor de Segovia* (The Weaver of Segovia) to Calderón de la Barca.

On page x of the prologue of his edition of two plays by Antonio García Gutiérrez (Clásicos Castellanos, volume 65, 1958), José Lomba y Pedraja points out that two foreigners, Carl August Regensburger and Nicholson B. Adams, find the *Trovador* to be based upon Larra's *Macías*, in turn taken from Lope de Vega's *Porfiar hasta morir*. Juan Alcina Franch in his *Teatro romántico* further elaborates this point. It is obvious that none of these critics has read all the plays they thus try to relate and that they have not tried to go beyond the dramatic piece to investigate the historical people portrayed in them. If there were a connection between the *Trovador* and *Macías*, Larra himself likely would have mentioned it. A love triangle is not unusual, in the theater or in real life, and the fact that Macías and Manrique were troubadours is not enough to trace García Gutiérrez's play to that source. Study of Larra's works leads to Macías and his poetry published in the *Cancionero de Baena*, and to Gonzalo Argote de Molina's account of the historic legend of Macías. The similarity between the two characters and the two plays is really almost nil.

Juan Alcina Franch agrees with most of the laudatory things others have to say about García Gutiérrez. Briefly, he refers to the novelty of having an author come up onstage to receive the acclaim of the public, unheard of in Spain until the debut of *El trovador*. He adds that in 1843, shortly before his departure for the New World, García Gutiérrez was crowned on stage with a laurel wreath after the first performance of *Simón Bocanegra*. Alcina repeats what others, notably Nicholson Adams, have said about similarities and influences, and cites gypsies in other plays. The text of *El trovador* which Alcina used in his 1968 edition is that of 1866 in *Obras escogidas*. Among other errors in this edition, possibly the printer's, we must add that no geographical location is given for the palace (mispelled) where the main action takes place, and that Guillén de Sesé is billed by Alcina as Leonor's father, when it is very clear they are brother and sister.

IV *Other Comments*

The spontaneity, freshness, and vitality of the early evaluations of García Gutiérrez and his *Trovador* stem from the fact that many who wrote such reviews and praise were his contemporaries, able to see the drama performed and to feel the emotional impact García Gutiérrez was so well equipped to work into his plays. Knowing the person and yet being unable to find fault with either the man or the artist is a rare thing indeed. With people so experienced in the field as Ferrer del Río and Cayetano Rosell, for instance, their judgment logically has to be more reliable than a later study, just as the word of an eyewitness outweighs circumstantial evidence. Larra alone would have sufficed to do justice to García Gutiérrez, with his lengthy review that had to be published in two parts. His presence in the theater and his easy pen captured every mood and word which other people, some of whom were also present that night, have repeated in more or less the same terms. The reading of the *Trovador* is sufficient proof of the excitement of that first performance.

All the critics mentioned have a specific purpose for their writings; their common denominator is agreement on the exquisite qualities of the dramatist García Gutiérrez and his first gem, the *Trovador*. Ferrer del Río gives a résumé of the writer's triumphs and general information about his environment, times, and contemporaries. Hartzenbusch, as one of the promoters of the collection honoring our author, expresses himself in similar terms and gives a complete, up-to-date list of García Gutiérrez's plays (to avoid repetition, much laudatory material must be eliminated). Cayetano Rosell, in charge of editing García Gutiérrez's work in the volume published by Novo y Colson, gives an evaluation of Romanticism and how it applies to the privileged case of García Gutiérrez, while Guaza, whose book deals with musicians, poets, and diverse artists, includes our author because so many talents converge within him in happy combination. His description of the dramatic impact the spectator experiences seems exaggerated, but it is not so in the case of García Gutiérrez. Nicholson Adams, first and foremost a scholar, evaluates the dramatic efforts of our author more as literature and something to be analyzed than as dramatic art. Not exempt from artistic perception by any means, his book nevertheless suffers from inaccuracies. Lomba y Pedraja, whose work in Clásicos Castellanos dates from 1958, had gathered all the material available and offers a panoramic history of the man and his works, but at times gives the impression of having repeated what others have said, rather than reading certain plays and judging for himself. His comments on *Venganza catalana* and *Juan Lorenzo* will be noted later. Juan Alcina has read all or most of the material already mentioned, adding his own comments or interpretations. With the wealth of material at his disposal, he has attempted to be as inclusive as possible and thus some mistakes and inaccuracies are found.

A curious work is that offered by Fr. Amado de Cristo Burguera y Serrano entitled *Representaciones escénicas malas, peligrosas y honestas* (Dramatic Performances, Bad, Dangerous and Honest), in three volumes. The first was published in Barcelona (1911); the second, termed a supplement, in Valencia (1915); also printed in Valencia in the same year is the third volume, which is a résumé of the preceeding two. In essence it contains a moral classification of several thousand dramatic works of various kinds, intended as a guide to good and decent Christians, especially men who wish to raise their families in a clean atmosphere, and above all directed to those ladies who in the morning go to church, and in the evening display themselves and their jewelry in the theater. The classification of plays recommended or given a bad rating is based on several premises, the most important of which is not the plot as a whole. The author calls attention to the fact that a seemingly innocent word or dialogue might contain double meaning, especially when aided by gestures and voice inflection not found on the written page. Many playwrights are condemned for their ideas, especially if they happen to be liberal or socialistic, or if they attack the church or clergy. Going back to ancient theater, Fr. Burguera traces and separates what was edifying and what was not, as well as the authors that tended to lean in one direction or another. The theater per se is not bad, he says, but can be because of what it can be made to suggest or exemplify, and above all because of the immediate effect it has on the audience.

In sum, Fr. Burguera's work intends to fight indecency. His ratings of plays are based not only on his own readings or firsthand

The First Play

experience, but on the judgment of scholars, historians, priests, and critics in books, magazines, and newspapers. In such instances the source is identified. While recognizing its value and good intentions, it must be noted that Fr. Burguera's work has faults that cannot be overlooked: many titles are ascribed to the wrong author, and at times the same play is accorded different ratings. This is the case of Antonio García Gutiérrez, to whom several titles by Juan Eugenio Hartzenbusch are attributed. There are too many cases for this to be an error, causing one to think that perhaps García Gutiérrez's popularity was such that often, without checking, a play was deemed to be his. In the specific case of *El trovador*, Fr. Burguera (taking as his authority Fr. Francisco Blanco García) describes it as a Romantic drama, repulsive and satanic. The Verdi version, however, is listed by Burguera simply as an opera in four acts which takes place in Aragon and Vizcaya, in the year 1409, among ladies, soldiers, and gypsies.

In a convention held recently by French Hispanists in Lille, observations concerning *El trovador* included the fact that it contains anachronisms in dress and buildings, and that the gypsies had not yet made their appearance in Spain in those times. However, more solid ground is needed to criticize a play that so appeals to emotions. Lacking specific information is also the note that an opera by Porcel based on *El trovador* was performed in Pamplona in 1842 and in Santiago the following year.

The Espasa-Calpe encyclopedia notes that García Gutiérrez took the uprising of the Count of Urgel and some names and dates from the historic accounts of Jerónimo Zurita in order to anchor his play, without paying attention to the environment or to verisimilitude. According to Covarrubias, the gypsies came to Europe in 1417, so that the play bearing as date "fifteenth century" seems to be in keeping with the times. I have not found the 1409 date Fr. Burguera mentions. Strangely enough, given the tragic plot of *El trovador*, García Gutiérrez wrote a parody of his own play titled *Los hijos del tío Tronera* (Uncle Tronera's Children) performed in 1849. The parody will be discussed in chapter four.

CHAPTER 3

The Theater of García Gutiérrez

I The Decade of 1830–1840

EL Page (The Page Boy) was first performed May 22, 1837, at the Príncipe Theater and published the same year in Madrid by Sancha. Acts one, two, and three take place in Córdoba, and the fourth, in Sevilla. The drama begins in the house of Don Martín de Sandoval, Count of Niebla, on March 20, 1369. Ferrando, a fifteen-year-old page, quarrels with an old servant, Bermudo, while playing cards. The page has a dagger his father gave him with words he did not understand about its being his destiny, but he would rather carry a sword. He challenges Bermudo to a duel which is stopped by Leonor, sister of the Countess, Blanca, who enters. It becomes evident Ferrando loves her. He is dismissed and Blanca tells Leonor she has seen Rodrigo, her old love, and fears he followed her; her husband the Count must not see him. Rodrigo enters and talks to Blanca, recalling their love. When she asks what became of the child they had, Rodrigo explains he had to abandon him when they parted because he was a fugitive from justice. He proposes they go together to Sevilla to look for the boy. Count Martín arrives and Rodrigo gives him letters from his brother to justify his presence there, but Bermudo recognizes Rodrigo as Blanca's former suitor and warns the Count, who does not want to know more about his wife's indiscretion. He is aware of Blanca's plan to meet Rodrigo that night, and he will be there.

Act two takes place at the inn where Rodrigo is staying. Leonor comes to ask him not to see Blanca, but he insists that his one-time lover, now Countess, betrayed him and subsequently plots with Farfán to kill his rival. Bermudo, entering, reveals he was a servant in the house of Blanca's father and knows about their love affair and much more; he then gives Rodrigo a key to Blanca's room. Scene five, in verse, shows Ferrando in the Countess's room, which has a window opening on the Guadalquivir River. The page is weeping as he sings a love song accompanied by his lute. Leonor enters and comments with him upon the pains of love, which have the young boy in constant unrest. Alone again, he soliloquizes concerning his love for Blanca, wondering what his mother would say if she saw her young son in that state. He repeats his plaint to Blanca, who sends him away and laments that she will not see Rodrigo again. When he appears she rejects him for fear of her husband, but she loves Rodrigo, and when he insists they regain what was lost, she capitulates. Just then Martín, Bermudo, and Farfán enter, and a fight ensues.

In act three Rodrigo, near Córdoba, encounters Nuño, a fugitive who does not hesitate to take money for an undisclosed service to be performed that night. He turns out to be the man Rodrigo set out to find, a fisherman to whom he entrusted his child fifteen years before. Nuño explains the baby was left next to a chapel when his money ran out; he became a bandit and his band is dispersed now. Rodrigo proposes that Nuño help him abduct a married woman. Back in the Count of Niebla's house, Fortún brings Ferrando news of the death of his father and a letter about his true origin. The page is dismayed to learn he was abandoned; at his cry Leonor comes to quiet him. Count Martín is wounded, as Ferrando can see when he lifts the tapestry concealing his bed from view. How did it happen? All Ferrando knows is that Bermudo died. Blanca enters, finding the boy in a sad state, and he tells her of his silent love. She takes pity on him and kisses his forehead, but that is worse, and he confesses that his love is for her. Blanca, surprised, tells him to be quiet: her love brings misfortune. As a signal is heard, Blanca struggles between her desire to go with Rodrigo and the duty to keep her vows as a wife. She tells the page to prove his love by stabbing Martín; it will then be legal for her to love him, since she will be a widow. Ferrando, horrified, rejects happiness at the price of someone's death. She spurs him on, swearing that she loves him. The page goes to Martín's bed and a scream is heard. As Rodrigo enters the page comes out, shaken, and sees the lovers leave. Plunging his dagger into the door they close behind them, he curses Blanca.

Act four is set in Sevilla, where Nuño comments upon the assassination of the Count of Niebla; his wife's page must have done it, because his dagger was found there. Ferrando, who has come from Córdoba with Antúnez, listens in hiding. Nuño says a fisherman (himself) was contracted to throw the dead man into the river, but he found the dagger in a door; the page should have kept it, because it was the only way his parents would be able to identify him. Later Ferrando speaks to Nuño, and discovers that Rodrigo de Vargas is his father, Blanca's lover. The old man agrees to bring them together, returning Ferrando's dagger. The page says he will not go to the house—rather, Rodrigo should meet him at the Triana bridge—and muses to himself that this way he can find Blanca alone. Nuño, at Rodrigo's house, tells him the boy does not want to come, and that he loves Blanca; does he not know she is his mother? Rodrigo leaves as the servants wonder where he is going on his wedding night.

Ferrando, after pleading with the servants to allow him to take shelter in the house, makes his way to Blanca's bedroom; he will die avenged. Recalling his painful love, her rejection, and the way she hurt him, he does not want that woman to take the place of his mother. He conceals himself as Blanca and her attendants enter, the ladies commenting on the death of the Count of Niebla behind her back. She orders them out, puzzled by Rodrigo's absence, and suddenly finding Ferrando in front of her she screams. His accusations are very strong and he wants to kill her. While in the next room the wedding feast and music are heard, Ferrando takes poison, speaking of her evil ways, and offers Blanca the phial. She pleads she does not want to lose her soul; the page tells her *she* lost *his*, but gives her time to pray. Meanwhile his rage subsides, and tells Blanca her beauty is her shield; he will die with his love and despair, while she will occupy his mother's bed, since Rodrigo is his father. Blanca is horrified to learn this, but the poison is taking effect and it is too late. Ferrando expires as Rodrigo enters, and kneeling by the boy, he rejects and curses Blanca, who has put a curse and a tomb between them.

The prose scenes are mainly of conspiracy, or ordinary talk. The language is especially lyric when the young page expresses his love, whether he is talking about it naming the subject, complaining of the suffering it inflicts, or conversing of love with Leonor, in terms which are delicate and extremely beautiful. Blanca emerges at first as a woman chained to a man she married unwillingly, torn between love and duty; however, her behavior later includes murder and hurting young Ferrando beyond his endurance. Her devious means bring unhappiness to everyone, and produce three deaths: those of Bermudo, the Count of Niebla, and Ferrando. The situation in which the page finds himself appeals exclusively to the emotions. The painful state of his hopeless love is followed by a deception which sinks him even further, since he has committed a crime for the woman he loves, who in turn has used him. Trying to protect someone who is not blameless, but who happens to be his father, from such an evil woman, adds to the boy's misfortune, since he has been informed only partially about Rodrigo and Blanca, and must trust what he sees. So many ills heaped upon one so young and innocent, in contrast with the immorality of some of the other characters, make the last part of this play a clamor for divine justice.

Enrique López Funes is repulsed by the subject of this play, blaming it on the French influences he detects, and dislikes the inappropriate language of Ferrando in one of the last scenes, since he is too young to speak as a mature man. Otherwise he praises the dialogue as a true wonder. Of Blanca he says she is motivated by sex only. Father Burguera, citing the opinion of Father Blanco, calls *El page* an exaggerated and impure drama, while Nicholson Adams compares *El page* to *The Tour de Nesle,* written in 1832 by Alexander Dumas, a play García Gutiérrez translated in cooperation with Isidoro Gil in 1836 as *Margarita de Borgoña. El page* (1837) is no doubt taken in part from the Dumas play, but exploring a different aspect of it. The story Buridan tells Margarita in scene four of act three provides the basis, but García Gutiérrez focuses his attention on the young page, making him the innocent prey of the woman who uses his feelings for her to her advantage. In the French play, Buridan (the young page) had enjoyed his love with Margarita to the point that she was about to give birth. At her instigation he killed Margarita's father to be free of his authority. The situation with Ferrando is quite different. Buridan takes a long time to find the woman who led him to commit a crime, and in the process he finds their twin sons, who are killed by order of their mother not in infancy as she thought, but as young men, one of them being one of her prospective lovers, as their identity was unknown to her. Buridan himself is not completely innocent, but compared to Margarita he is a hero. The last criticism, that of Alcina, repeats others, stating that *El page* was not well received in the theater because of its unsavory theme.

II El rey monge (*The Monk King*)

A verse drama in five acts, *El rey monge* was written in 1837 (published in Madrid by Yenes in 1839), with no information concerning the first performance. It takes place in Monzón, Aragon, in the twelfth century. Act one, "The Meeting," transpires during the festivities of King Alfonso and Queen Urraca's wedding, as Ramiro, the King's brother, bemoans his lot; he was sent in childhood to a monastery. He loves Isabel, who returns his feelings without knowing his identity. Alfonso, leaving for Huesca, sends word to Ramiro that he has decided to send him as abbot to Sahagún, and Ramiro plans to see his lady love that night.

In the first part of act two, "The Rope Ladder," Ramiro at Isabel's window plans to ask her father for her hand, but insists on keeping his identity secret. She retires, but her maid lets Ramiro in as Ferriz, Isabel's father, arrives, being stopped in the street by Ortiz, Ramiro's servant, who dies in an ensuing fight. Aldonza, Isabel's maid, warns her mistress, and Ramiro flees. In the second part, "Dead for the World," Aldonza is confronted with her treason and Ferriz wants to punish her by death; Isabel will be dead to the world, but the casket leaving the house will contain the body of the traitor Aldonza. Ramiro arrives, asking for Isabel in arrogant and insolent terms; Ferriz answers by pointing to another room where she presumably is, in a casket with four candles.

In the third act, "The Bishop of Roda," Ramiro reminisces about his lost love Isabel, her bier, and the world he never enjoyed. The abbot and a friar bring him news of his brother Alfonso's death; Ramiro is now the only heir to the throne, which he had wanted only for Isabel. A group of noblemen, among them Don Ferriz, arrive to ask Ramiro to occupy the throne. Ferriz recognizes his offender and refuses to kiss his hand. The other are scandalized, but Ramiro forgives him. However, Ferriz agitates the other gentlemen by hinting that the new king will be a tyrant. Although he does not reveal the nature of the offense against him, they plot to avenge the old man, since his son is not back from the war. In the fourth act, "An Orgy" is held in the castle of Don Ferriz. After a banquet with fellow conspirators, two more, blindfolded, are brought in. While the others sleep it is revealed they are loyal to the king. One is Alfonso, the son of Don Ferriz. They want to warn Ramiro but do not know where they are. Isabel appears like a vision, delirious, dressed in white; she tells her brother of her forced seclusion and the pain she suffers, caused by the love of a man she does not know. Asking Alfonso for help she goes back to her room without further explanation.

Don Ferriz enters and, finding his son, urges him to avenge Isabel's honor. Voices and noise indicate that the castle is being invaded, and soldiers surround the conspirators. Isabel tries unsuccessfully to prevent her father from being apprehended. "The Bell of Huesca," second part of the fourth act, takes place in a square of that city before the palace of King Ramiro, who is ready to bring the traitors to justice. The bells announce the execution of two of them. The king says he is fulfilling his promise to cast a bell from the heads of the traitors as a lesson to those who plan to rebel; next to be executed is Don Ferriz. Isabel appears, imploring clemency, but Ramiro, always haunted by her voice, leaves, since he believes she is dead.

Act five, "The Confession," occurs in the monastery of St. Peter the Elder, in Huesca. The abbot and a monk comment on Fray Ramiro's illness; he is in deep sorrow, fasting, wears a hair shirt and prays constantly because of his misdeeds, refusing to cure his ills. The abbot's attempt to talk with him fails as he is intent only on his sorrow. Having lost hope, he cannot thank God for sending him trials superior to his strength. Why do so many have beautiful and pleasant lives, and he cannot; the bright spot Isabel could have been for him was lost, and he is in a living hell. A veiled woman enters seeking confession, and Ramiro sits in the confessional. The woman confesses being dishonored by a man she loved, for whom she prays in her inability to forget him, even though it eventually cost her father his life. Ramiro says there is no offense to God if she was seduced and prayed ever after; he also loved and suffered because of a brief meeting with his lady love. Asking who she is, he reveals his face to her; she is Isabel, and sees that the confessor is Ramiro. Realizing that her death was a falsehood, he curses her father. She wants to be with Ramiro, but he rejects her; his life has been flickering for days and he feels death approaching, yet he can think only of her, not of eternity. Ramiro leaves for his cell forbidding Isabel to follow him, but she insists on being with him to be the first to mourn his death. Alfonso and a companion arrive, the former seeking to challenge Ramiro as a monk, since he was one when he sentenced his father. Finding his sister Isabel there makes him more indignant; Ramiro has expired, and she asks Alfonso to kill her. He refuses, preferring to let her live and weep, and to leave to God the avenging of Don Ferriz.

Each act is preceded by a title indicating the main theme, which sets the mood. At the beginning we see Ramiro is unhappy with his monkish state, forced upon him by his father. His determination to enter Isabel's room and subsequent request that she be given to him clashes with his religious condition, as also happens when he brings the conspirators to justice. His religious dedication comes from a fear of God rather than from deep belief; his behavior is that of a frustrated man, but not intended as condemnation of the religious life. The last act constitutes an outpouring of the anguish in which some people exist, compounded by actions and circumstances over which they have no control. Explanations that could change a life are missing, and when Isabel reveals similar feelings and guilt, the father seems less of a victim. Alfonso, as a marginal character, entrusted with restoring the family honor, cannot appraise the harm done his sister by lack of dialogue with her father. Ramiro expires while Isabel endures life, yet both have been dead inside for a long time. Even the most distasteful scenes in the dubious story of King Ramiro are handled by García Gutiérrez in straightforward fashion, and the characters are consistent throughout.

Historically, King Ramiro II, the Monk, was placed in a monastery in childhood, possibly in 1093, and subsequently forced to occupy the throne at the death of his brother Alfonso I, the Fighter (Batallador), in 1134, since he was the only heir. In 1136 he married Inés de Poitiers, by whom he had a daughter, Petronila. Once the child was bethrothed, in infancy, to Ramón Berenguer IV, Count of Barcelona, the king abdicated the throne on her behalf, and, in 1137, returned to the monastery. Petronila and Count Berenguer were married in 1151. During his brief rule legend says that King Ramiro, due to his monastic life, was not ready to govern and was not taken seriously by influential members of the nobility, to such an extreme that the king decided to make an example of them in the episode of the casting of the bell of Huesca. Some historians contend this is sheer invention, not found in written accounts until the mid-fifteenth century.

Enrique López Funes states that *El rey monge* was performed for the first time in the Príncipe Theater of Madrid, December 18, 1837, and later in every Spanish theater, as was *El trovador*. López

Funes defends the monologues (criticized by those who contend that nobody talks to himself), affirming that the inner life is a perpetual monologue. He laments that no actor can do justice to the role of Ramiro after the death of Pedro González Mate (an actor from Cádiz). López Funes concurs that Ramiro does not protest against the law that made him a monk because of ambition for power, but rather yearning for the freedom to love.

Marcelino Menéndez y Pelayo, with his biting tongue, finds fault with García Gutiérrez's play, viewing it solely as a Romantic effort by an inexperienced dramatist. Perhaps his praising the lyricism and criticizing the "infantile psychology and thin line" prevented other critics from taking note of the play. Menéndez y Pelayo appears incapable of thinking in terms of human feelings, the major theme of most Romantics. García Gutiérrez's play cannot be called a disservice to the royal person he portrays since above and beyond any real happenings and a historic setting, aside from any drastic and barbaric actions triggered by anger (as is the case with Don Ferriz in the first act), the spiritual turmoil of Ramiro and the plight of Isabel overpower everything, including the so-called inaccuracies. García Gutiérrez did as most dramatists both before and after him, bringing to his contemporary audience human passions and conflicts, anchoring his tale in a few strategic points, not staging passages taken straight from a history book. The human being, not the king or the monk, is given his day on stage. Father Burguera reflects the opinion of Catholic magazines in rating this play "sacrilegious."

III Magdalena

Magdalena is an 1837 drama in five acts, in verse and in prose, which did not obtain the necessary license to be performed; nevertheless it was published by Repullés in 1837 and again in 1844. The first two acts take place in Madrid, the others in Guadalajara, although due to an obvious misprint the opposite is indicated. Magdalena and her brother, Fernando, were taken in by Doña Juana when they were orphaned. The girl loves Doña Juana's son, Carlos. Fernando, about to leave for war in Navarra, entrusts his honor to her, saying the man she loves is no good and has taken her for granted. Braulia, a servant, advises Magdalena to go to the masked ball and observe Carlos. The latter enters with Julián, remarking with disgust that Magdalena is everywhere. Doña Juana announces the imminent wedding of Carlos to Adela, a marchioness, and he changes the subject. Fernando departs after entrusting his sister and her honor to Carlos. Magdalena, enraged at the news of the engagement, decides to attend the ball.

Act two opens in the ballroom; Magdalena, dressed as a vestal virgin, attracts Carlos, who believes her to be Adela. Soon he is disappointed to discover he has been courting Magdalena, while Adela is most annoyed at the confusion. Both women leave him, in a rage. Act three finds Braulia and Julián preparing for the wedding of Carlos and Adela, in her small house in a village near Guadalajara. A year has elapsed and Magdalena has been missing since the night of the ball. All go to church except Doña Juana, who receives the surprise visit of Fernando, and must inform him of the wedding and Magdalena's absence. Act four takes place outside the church of St. Gil, where we see the wedding party, guests, and townspeople bearing torches and flowers. Fernando writes a note challenging Carlos to a duel the next morning, and finds a way to convey it to him in church. Magdalena, with her previously unmentioned three-year-old daughter, Amelia, stops to beg next to the church and her brother recognizes her. When the wedding party comes out, Carlos is startled to see Magdalena, who faints upon recognizing him.

Act five shows the humble abode of Agueda, who took in Magdalena and her child out of pity. Carlos appears seeking Magdalena, who is asleep; when Braulia also comes he asks not to be seen. Braulia tells Magdalena that Fernando is wounded; he will see her when he has recovered, then she and Amelia can live with him. Magdalena professes her undying love for Carlos, who reveals his presence when Braulia leaves. He is repentant, but too late; his presence will make Magdalena's life even harder. Carlos insists he may die soon and asks to kiss the sleeping Amelia. Magdalena realizes he is suffering and wonders if he may try to take the girl away from her; entering to see her daughter she finds a letter from Carlos saying he is going to fight a duel with Fernando, and in case he dies he wills all he has to Amelia. When Fernando later announces that he has cleansed his honor and that of Magdalena by killing Carlos, she is neither relieved nor happy, as she would not have been had the reverse happened. Fernando tells Amelia she has a father in him.

A pure melodrama, this five-act play seems at times more like a novel. Carlos is depicted as a selfish man, unaffected by the pain he causes others, while Magdalena is portrayed as a poor, unlucky, and unhappy girl. She is a long-suffering, rejected mother whose undying love for Carlos makes her life miserable, but she is hardly without blame. It is not clear how she could bear a child and hide that fact from Doña Juana, in whose house she lived, or from her brother. Braulia seems too opinionated and disrespectful for her condition as servant, especially considering the language she uses to criticize Julián. A curious commentary that reveals some of the thinking of García Gutiérrez is found in act three, when Braulia complains that she will suffocate in the small town; she would give anything for a bit of the Prado, or a first-row seat in the Príncipe Theater (not the Cruz, since she does not go that far in her enjoyment of theater); in the village she complains there is nowhere to go for a walk, and not one Romantic play to be seen.[1] Fr. Blanco, according to Fr. Burguera, qualified *Magdalena* as a filthy play; rejected by the censors, it was never performed. Nicholson Adams also quotes Fr. Blanco.

IV El bastardo *(The Bastard)*

El bastardo, a verse drama in five acts, was published by Piñuela (Madrid, 1838). There are no references to performance, or to place and time when the play occurs. As the first act opens, Pedro de Sessé visits Count Bernardo to tell him their children cannot marry; Ramiro is not his son, and his low birth is not worthy of Elvira, therefore, they dissolve the engagement. The King summons father and son to his palace in Nájera (Navarra), so Pedro tells Ramiro that he is not his son and he must go to serve the King. The young man declares he loves a woman he met after Elvira; unable to face his fiancée, he gives her maid, Inés, the message that he has gone to find out the real name of his father. Upon receipt of this news Elvira weeps. Act two opens in the palace of the King of Navarra. Prince Don García and Nuño follow a mysterious lady who avoids them; they see Ramiro, famous for his good traits and valor, and decide to keep him away since he can be competition. Queen Leonor seems to be Ramiro's lady love, and she leaves when the mysterious woman appears again. It is Elvira, who demands to know why Ramiro has jilted her; she has seen the Queen there but will keep quiet about that. When García and Nuño approach, Ramiro defends Elvira, who does not want to reveal her face. García and Ramiro draw their swords, and Elvira leaves. The King is announced, scolds both youths, and sends Ramiro out of the room. He reveals to García that Ramiro is also his son, but he will not be told until he proves himself worthy. García complains that too many of his brothers may wear the crown, including a bastard.

In act three the King and his men prepare to leave for Córdoba to fight the Moors, while the Queen, in a soliloquy, reveals she is quite attracted to Ramiro. Don Pedro de Sessé suspects the cause of her sadness, which he believes the King should know, and tell Ramiro who he is. Count Bernardo arrives in search of his daughter, suspecting her to be with Ramiro. García, previously intent only on having a good time, resolves to get rid of his half-brother, and others who stand in his way. He accuses Don Pedro and the Queen of being lovers, and the courtiers surround them. In act four Queen Leonor has issued an edict that she not be judged until the return of the King, who has been recalled. García demands immediate punishment for her, but the courtiers ask him to prove her guilt. When King Sancho arrives, García swears that the Queen dishonored him, and she is surrounded. Leonor says that defending herself from a falsehood would degrade her; her only crime is having given birth to a monster: García. All agree that she must be guilty except for Ramiro, who challenges García to prove what he says; they will fight a duel.

In act five the imprisoned Queen bemoans her lot and hopes for a painless death. Ramiro comes to tell her he will not kill García, only extract from him a retraction. Tello brings news that García is missing and that the King wants to see Ramiro. Elvira, disguised as a page, enters to see Leonor, and explains her plight. The two women understand each other without using names. The King, Don Pedro, Ramiro, and the courtiers appear to proclaim the innocence of the Queen, after which the King reveals that Ramiro is his illegitimate son; Leonor will be his mother. When Count Bernardo arrives demanding justice, the Queen decrees that Ramiro and Elvira should marry and occupy the throne of Aragon. Sancho challenges his men to fight the Moors or leave his kingdom.

As in many historical plays, there is a mixture of elements inherited from Golden Age theatrical productions: the fathers are old and decrepit, while their children are very young. Love at first sight dominates more than one soul. The Queen is young and beautiful, although she has grown sons. The mere hint of impropriety is deemed a dishonor to husband or father, but everyone keeps his place in the end, while nursing incurable psychic wounds. *The Bastard* is based on a more or less fictitious episode in the life of King Sancho III of Navarra (1000–1035), who had three legitimate children and one illegitimate son, Ramiro. García Gutiérrez is by no means the only author to touch upon such themes. López Funes regrets not having had access to this play; other critics do not even mention it.

V Samuel

Samuel (published by Repullés, 1839) is another drama for which there is no information concerning performance. Of the four acts, in verse and prose, the first three occur in Sevilla, the last in Ecija, in 1278. As the play opens Alfonso and Enrique serenade Ester in the dark street of the Jewish quarter of Sevilla, to her delight, although she stays out of sight. At dawn Samuel visits his neighbor Isaac, asking him to spy on the men who so often visit the street, since he suspects they are attracted to his young wife, Ester. Maybe they were better off in Granada; thirty years before he had buried his treasures in Sevilla when he found an underground passage under his house.[2] Returning to retrieve his treasure, he finds that the house now belongs to Don Pedro de Vargas, to whose son Enrique Samuel has lent money before. His other reason for returning to Sevilla is to seek revenge on those who killed his wife and son.

Enrique asks Samuel for another loan, but the old man wants more than his word or signature as collateral; he ends up giving money to Enrique when the latter assures Samuel that he will inherit the next day, since his father is old and sick. Alfonso criticizes Enrique's carefree behavior and his love for a married Jewess, whose husband he does not know. Alfonso opposes Enrique's abducting Ester, but agrees to help his friend that night. Isaac overhears them, disapproves of the plan, and tells Samuel. Act two takes place in Ester's house. Enrique is seen in the balcony, then hiding behind the draperies, as Ester and her maid, Rebeca, enter the room and talk about the old husband and the young admirer. Ester points out, however, that their religions are different and she cannot dishonor her husband, who arrives home earlier than usual. Samuel notes that she is much younger; he had cared for her when she was left alone, having lost her family; now she is his life. She reflects that respect is not love and confesses she loves someone else, but will remain loyal to Samuel. He wants to kill the man; then he decides they must leave Sevilla at once. Ester laments her lot, and opens the balcony, finding Enrique, who tells her of his love. Replying that she cannot love him because she is married, she even calls Samuel, but Enrique locks the door and, aided by his friends, takes Ester away.

In act three Samuel and Isaac enter the patio of Don Pedro de Vargas's house via the underground passage shortly before Enrique and the others enter by another door, with Ester unconscious. When she revives Ester begs Enrique to take her back to her husband. She now despises Enrique because Samuel will not believe her loyalty. Enrique suggests that if she were a Christian they could be married; she first rejects the idea, but reconsiders, as a means to be free of Samuel's wrath. As Samuel is heard calling Ester, Alfonso is entrusted to take her to Ecija; that way he can inquire what Samuel is doing at that hour of night in his father's house. The old Jew wastes no time or words, but Enrique claims to be his long-lost son. As they embrace for the second time, Enrique holds a dagger in his hand. The carriage with Ester and the trusted men is seen and Samuel wants to go to his wife, but the wily Enrique now tells him that his father Don Pedro de Vargas is his enemy; he only wanted to test Samuel's credibility.

In the fourth act, in Ecija, Ester tells Enrique that she has had bad dreams, and he comments that this is the voice of her conscience. While disloyal to Samuel, she finds it hard to take accusations from Enrique, who receives a letter informing him of his father's death. Don Pedro's dying wish was for Enrique to honor his plan to marry a certain rich lady. Ester senses she is being abandoned and is sad. Isaac and Samuel finally succeed in finding her after a servant of Enrique, threatened with death, revealed her whereabouts. Samuel forgives her but wants to kill Enrique; his father had led the men who killed Samuel's family while driving the Moors out of Sevilla. Enrique finds Samuel determined to kill him; after harsh words they draw their swords and Enrique falls, mortally wounded. Ester faints, but utters Samuel's name and he knows she is his forever.

Enrique is insulting to the Jews from the start, more for their traits than for their religion, and his plans are hampered by the reluctance and resistance of Ester, who loves him, but when illicit happiness is at her door realizes it cannot exist without clouds overshadowing it. Samuel hesitates between guarding his wife and recovering his treasure, bent on a revenge he took too long to pursue. He kills Enrique more for what his father did in battle than for having taken his wife, Ester, who was not without fault, not exactly a victim in the entire affair. While it is not surprising that Samuel forgives her, since she has learned a lesson, his killing Enrique for what he has not done makes his revenge less justifiable. López Funes considers *Samuel* more a product resulting from the action than from a calculated plot, but very effective as theater. For López Funes, Ester is driven by a physiological force; he dislikes Vargas, but credits García Gutiérrez with not making Samuel ridiculous.

CHAPTER 4

The Decade 1840–1850

I El Encubierto de Valencia
(*The Disguised Man of Valencia*)

EL Encubierto de Valencia, a verse drama in five acts, was performed at the Príncipe Theater in Madrid on July 17, 1840, and published by Rivadeneyra the same year. The first act takes place in the house of the Marquis of Cenete, magistrate of Orán. His daughter Blanca listens as María yearns for her distant and sunny Spain. The man María loves is in Orán, but does not notice her; it is Enrique, brought up with her as brother and sister; he courts Blanca, but her father opposes the match because he is of humble origin. Juan de Bilbao, whom Enrique calls "father," arrives with news from Spain: the communal revolution is spreading. The Marquis opposes the guilds, while Juan sees nothing wrong with their claim. Later he tells Enrique he is to head the rebels in Valencia. The young man is happy to go; his ambition is greater than his love for Blanca. The Marquis receives orders to head the forces of the king against the guilds, so he and Enrique will be in opposite sides. He will not let their friendship interfere. When they part, the Marquis orders the captain to apprehend Enrique and Juan de Bilbao. María overhears and goes to warn both men.

In act two, later, in the town hall of Valencia, María confides to her father, Juan de Bilbao, that she loves Enrique, who is indifferent to her. Blanca's father, the Marquis of Cenete, tries to sway Enrique's loyalty and Juan de Bilbao overhears the end of the conversation. The guilds, carrying their banners, enter, led by Juan Périz and Vicente Ruiz, two of the rebels. (This scene contains specific information as to what the banners should look like, identifying the various trades with appropriate symbols and their patron saint.) All kneel as Juan de Bilbao prays and proclaims Enrique their leader. Invoking the Cid and St. James, they go fight the enemy, already at the door.

Act three opens in a jail in Játiva, where Enrique is imprisoned. The Marquis of Cenete tries to explain to him that Castile is the deciding factor in his cause; after all, Padilla, Bravo, and Maldonado died. The Marquis receives word that the rebels are on their way to Játiva to free their leader; Juan de Bilbao must be there already, undercover. The captain is ordered to let anyone who so desires see Enrique, so he can spy on him. María comes to try to save Enrique, who fails to grasp her suffering. Juan de Bilbao interrupts, disguised as a monk. Before he frees Enrique he must make a confession: Juan took with him an abandoned child he found in Salamanca, next to the palace; the Marquis, listening from hiding, appears, to reveal that Enrique is the grandson of King Ferdinand and Queen Isabela, the legitimate heir to the Spanish throne, Juan III. Enrique, astonished, wants the power due him, and abandons Juan in favor of an alliance with the Marquis. Father and daughter are hurt; he wants revenge; she wants his forgiveness.

Act four finds a defeated and repentant Enrique in Valencia, in the house of Juan de Bilbao. He professes to want to marry María, who now mistrusts him; what he really wants is the paper proving his birth so that he can show it to Cardinal Pedro de Mendoza, but he tells María that he only wants to destroy it. She knows the location, but the cabinet that contains it is locked; Enrique plans to come back that night to get it. Juan has neglected María lately, but, as he puts it, she is his daughter, while Spain is his mother. When the girl leaves, Juan takes out the document and retires for the night. María awaits Enrique to give him the paper he needs, but instead he sneaks in to steal it, accompanied by the Marquis; María overhears them discuss a plan to ambush the rebels, and how Enrique will ask for Blanca's hand once he is king. María screams, and the sound of a body falling is heard. Juan finds her unconscious. When she revives and warns her father of his danger, he reveals that the document is in his hands. She cannot stop Enrique from marrying Blanca, but it will not be as king: she reads the document and burns it. It was written on July 8, 1497, by Margarita of Flanders, afraid of her jealous husband. Juan de Bilbao enters, sword in hand, pursued by Enrique and his men; María asks him to flee and stands by the doorway with a dagger to stop the traitors. When she shows Enrique the ashes, the Marquis, lacking the conclusive proof the document could provide, imprisons Enrique, to María's despair.

Act five takes place in a dungeon in Valencia, where Enrique ponders his life and actions, his ungratefulness and ambition. The Marquis comes to tell him he regrets the situation, but without proof of his birth he cannot save him. Both go to hear the sentence. When Enrique comes back, certain he will be executed, he finds María, who has bribed a jailer to set him free. He takes her presence as an insult, and has very harsh words for her, her father, and their humble origin. She tells him how she tried to bribe the judges, to no avail; however, the jailer has a ship ready, and she will stay in Valencia and see him no more. Then Enrique humbles himself before her. Another prisoner is brought in, Juan de Bilbao. After much arguing Juan refuses to leave with a traitor; only one can be saved, not both. María must choose between her father or the man she loves. Torn by the anguish of a decision which will hurt her either way, she leaves with her father as Enrique pleads in desperation. Those who will lead him to the scaffold appear at the door as the play ends.

Enrique is devious, ungrateful, and ambitious, in part because of his mysterious origin, with royal blood latent in his veins. María is one of those strong women García Gutiérrez depicts so well, shattered by her feelings, yet made to suffer even more because of her goodness and loyalty, pulled in opposite directions by her onesided passion and her filial duty. Enrique pays in an indirect way for his ill treatment of those who raised him and therefore love him. Juan suceeds in his defense of the guilds, but María gains nothing; her pain is augmented at every turn.

Antonio Ferrer del Río opines that the play declines dramatically somewhat when María hesitates between saving her father or Enrique. Carlos Guaza repeats that observation. However, both critics agree that the lyric vein and dramatic qualities are of such value that it would be picayunish to look for imperfections or to try to criticize the play. It must be observed that María tried to save Enrique in the first place, promising not to see him again, motivated purely by real love; she would have succeeded had he not been so bitter, wasting precious time insulting her, instead of letting her speak. The arrival of Juan de Bilbao as prisoner is totally accidental, so it is not unnatural for María to need time to overcome the shock of having to decide the fate of the two men she loved the most. Somewhat unsubstantially, another critic, Cayetano Rosell, says that Enrique embodies the bad influence of the French Naturalist school.

The political aspect of the play is historic. Enrique was in fact the son of Prince Juan and his wife, Margarita of Flanders, and although he could not prove his origin, he was known to posterity as the "rei encobert" (disguised or undercover king). Enrique made his appearance in Valencia in late 1521, when the communal wars were coming to an end with the rebel defeat. The "undercover king" helped prolong the war under the guise of expelling those Moors still in the region. Some members of the nobility set afire a house where defenders of the guild had gathered. Later, in 1522, Enrique was found in Burjasot, a small town near Valencia, and killed. In December of that year, after Játiva fell, Cardinal Diego Hurtado de Mendoza, better equipped to govern Christendom than a country in war, entered Valencia as viceroy. Pedro González de Mendoza, also a cardinal, had helped deceive Margarita of Flanders pretending she gave birth to a girl who died soon after, since the child was born after the death of his father; thus, the Archduke Philip of Austria would be proclaimed heir to the throne.[1]

Undoubtedly García Gutiérrez incorporated the love intrigue to reflect some aspects of the communal uprising, as well as the duplicity and despotism of the protagonist, Enrique, although in part forced into such a situation by being an unrecognized legitimate heir to the throne of Spain. The playwright thus could also show some of the responsibilities the Marquis of Cenete had, and the latter's difficult position in a situation he did not fully grasp (he was the brother of the viceroy).

II Los desposorios de Inés *(The Wedding of Ines)*

Similarly lacking information concerning its having been performed, *Los desposorios de Inés* is another 1840 verse drama in three acts. Published by Albert in the same year, it occurs in Sevilla. Simón, a butler, admits Ana (under the name of Isabel) to serve Inés. Her widowed mother, Leonor, wants Inés to marry Don Juan, because they are indebted to him. The girl resents having to pay debts that way, especially since she loves another, who is at war in Flanders, whether or not he returns her feelings. To this, Leonor says she can abandon her mother to die. Of course Inés agrees to obey her mother. Afterwards Simón, who has been listening, tells Leonor that Inés and Juan do not love each other; he further implies Inés is his daughter. Juan is not disappointed because Inés does not love him, but he wants to hear it from her lips. Inés obliges and Juan confesses he loved her at one time, but no more; they can marry, but not a tear for her absent love. A blow on the window, and a man seen standing with his back to the iron grill, make Inés believe her beloved has returned. Everyone is ready for the wedding but Inés feels feverish. Leonor is left alone and Félix, who enters, inquiring, wants to stop the ceremony, even though Leonor says Inés has forgotten him. Simón reasures Félix that is not so, and brings Ana out, to the astonishment of both.

Act two opens in Don Juan's house, in Inés's room Ana is startled to see that Juan is the bridegroom. During a respite from the party, Inés tells her mother what she thinks of her being sold that way, affirming that Leonor will cry for having done it. Leonor leaves Ana to keep Inés company; she falls asleep and Félix comes in. Ana hides and witnesses how Félix says words of love to Inés, who then awakens. She says she is being forced to marry, but let people talk; they love each other. Juan enters, ready to fight a duel with Félix, who is taken away by servants. Confronting Inés Juan informs her he will kill Félix and make her life miserable. She begs Juan to kill her, and as he lifts his dagger to oblige, Ana appears and stops him; as Inés faints, Juan runs off with Ana. In act three Inés recovers in confusion, summons Simón and asks him to alert Félix to meet her that night at her former house. When Leonor stops her, Inés tells her mother how much she hates her, and reveals Juan and Ana's running away together.

In Leonor's house, Juan explains to Ana that he left her for dead years before, and demands to know who was the man who entered her room. She answers that she does not know. Juan leaves her locked in while he unravels a certain mystery. Simón enters, keeping watch, and when his light goes out, Inés arrives while Ana knocks at her door, and is ignored. Juan returns and Inés, mistaking him for Félix, pleads with him not to risk his life. Juan reveals his identity and wants to take her with him, but Inés refuses unless he respects Félix's life. As Simón shields Inés from Juan, Félix arrives to witness these events, further complicated when Ana is allowed to appear. Then a series of secrets are brought out into the open:

Juan had earlier married Ana; her brother Félix, a captain with the army away at Flanders, thinking his sister had dishonored him, tried to kill her. Juan did not know the man he saw was her brother. When Leonor enters, everything is straightened out, except that Inés does not find out that Simón is her father, although she considers him as one because of his behavior toward her. From the start the intrigue and secrecy are maintained in the best tradition of a cape and sword play.

López Funes is displeased by this play to the point that he postulates a hand other than that of García Gutiérrez in the mysterious comings and goings, the presence of Ana, and the blind humility of Simón, despite the fact that it contains beautiful verses and the concept (often expressed by García Gutiérrez) of the sacrifice of the weak, and his strong protest.

III El caballero de industria (*The Cunning Gentleman*)

A verse comedy in three acts, *El caballero de industria* was performed with great success in the Madrid theaters (no specific date given) and published by Lalama in 1841. The play takes place in a garden at a time undisclosed. In act one Adela scolds her beloved Facundo for coming from Cádiz to Chiclana not really to see her, but her sister Filomena, whom Facundo says he finds boring because of her lofty thoughts and poetry; he loves Adela, and as a token of her love he demands a diamond ring that once belonged to her mother. The young man is in financial straits, so Adela is not sure the jewel is safe in his hands. As she goes to awaken her father, since it is almost noon, Catalina, the maid, tells Facundo he has a rival, old and vain Don Cucufate. Facundo discloses that he really wants Filomena, but as her cousin Florentin is always around her, he must bribe Catalina to aid him. However, he is short of money at the moment. Filomena enters speaking in poetic terms (regardless of what she says), and Facundo answers in kind.

Cucufate and Florentin return from a hunt; they seem very refined in a somewhat ridiculous way. Mentioning the continuous presence of Facundo, Florentín suggests that Cucufate should fight a duel with him to ensure that he leave Adela alone, but Cucufate disagrees—he is not in the military. Ceferino, the girls' father, joins the conversation. The other men complain about Facundo, noble but poor, mooching all the time, while Ceferino defends him. In the last scene Cucufate asks Catalina to declare his love to Adela for him; he is willing to bypass many girls who would like to marry him, including a woman recently widowed.

In the second act Cucufate inquires of Catalina how his suit is coming; Facundo overhears derogatory words about himself, including that he is not trustworthy. Coming out of hiding, he confronts Cucufate, who protests he was only joking; he leaves after threatening words from Facundo, who then gossips with Catalina about Ceferino, obsessed with his own nobility. Filomena enters, still with her lofty thoughts; Facundo confesses his love for her after she mentions Adela, momentarily coming down from the clouds. In ornate and florid tones Filomena professes to return his feelings, but her father wants her to marry Florentín, her cousin. Cucufate and Florentín discover the couple, and in very strong language disapprove of the match, making for a very funny scene where the menacing and angry words of the men contrast, in very sharp and colloquial language, with Filomena's still ornate and melodramatic expression. Her father comes to see what the trouble is, and she goes away to weep under a cork tree. When Ceferino, in very down-to-earth words, inquires what is going on, he is anwered in the same manner. The old man dismisses Florentín and Cucufate, enumerating their defects with Facundo, who, to his credit, even has a portrait of Hernán Cortés. They go off to have a drink together. Thereafter, Adela elicits information from Catalina, in the interest of landing Facundo, whom she has the maid summon. Confronted with his deceit, he pretends it is a misunderstanding: she is the one who is offending him by having another suitor, and liking it. She believes him, while in an aside he hopes she does not discover his lies.

In the third act Filomena, speaking in her accustomed poetic images, which very much annoy Catalina, inquires about Facundo's tardiness, in beautiful verses. The maid shows Facundo how to reach Filomena's balcony while he flatters her, speaking next to Filomena in the same poetic way, to propose that they go away together. He waits on the ladder, in an uncomfortable position, while she brings some jewels they can sell. Catalina, who happens by, makes fun of his predicament. When Filomena returns, further images of bucolic love are evoked by both lovers, but Cucufate, fighting off the mosquitoes, catches them by surprise. Removing the ladder, he leaves Facundo hanging from the balcony, and shouts for Florentín. Ceferino orders Cucufate to replace the ladder and not to tinker with nobility. Adela, who comes out to investigate, is informed in very precise, sarcastic, and humorous terms. Adela, quick-thinking, says Facundo seduced her, thereby adding to the confusion. Filomena is enraged, as is Ceferino, but she defends Facundo saying he only has that fault. Her father disagrees, concluding that noble and innocent Facundo has seduced both girls; he then orders the other noisy men to be quiet and to lock Facundo into one of the rooms. Filomena laments her lot; she will never complain about Facundo. Ceferino wants to summon the town magistrate, but Florentín convinces him to leave the mess alone, lest his honor suffer. Cucufate and Florentín want to kill Facundo, who wants to recover his honor. All eventually retrieve their money and jewels from the betrayer, who is ordered to leave. Everyone ends up unmarried, since the girls, as well as the two men, reject Ceferino's proposed arrangements. Florentín inquires if he is wiser now, advising his uncle to look more at the man as a whole, not just his titles.

El caballero de industria is a play full of elements worth studying. The types, the names, the descriptions, and the actions of the characters can be appreciated by a variety of people, taking into account such differences as age and degree of culture. Adela, ostentatious, jealous of the chiseler Facundo, whom she loves but knows is not to be trusted, is wooed both by him and Cucufate, an old and conceited gentleman. She pursues Facundo to the extreme of claiming he violated her, in order to provoke a quick reaction on the part of her father, who in turn will request an immediate marriage, but her scheme does not work. Filomena, lost in her imaginary world of poetry and metaphor, applies lyricism to the most ordinary things, and descends from her clouds only to fight for her beloved Facundo, whose duplicity and cunning she is willing to overlook. Catalina, a stereotyped maid, looks out for herself; she has information and opinions about everything, and her loyalty is measured by the reward involved. Facundo, a charmer, lives off others and does not hesitate either to take or to ask for whatever will increase his fortune. He declares his love to both sisters and even makes a pass at the maid, takes full advantage of Ceferino's preoccupation with names, titles of nobility, and social status. Cucufate, burdened with a comic-sounding name, is neither a dandy nor a Harlequin, but in his vanity and pride he believes himself to be a ladies' man, unaware of his ridiculous claims. Not a violent man, he professes enough energy to lick an army or whatever annoys him. Florentín, sure of his triumph over the other men because he is unlike them, and not musty as his uncle, urges everyone else to use fists and swords to solve problems, but, like the others, his pride is hurt when things become too tangled to unravel.

An illiterate person can enjoy the portrayal of those characters and situations in the same way that a scholar can detect the playwright's poking fun at old traditions, obsolete customs, excessive pride, nobility, melodrama, idealistic love, and other assorted prejudices. Additional aspects can, no doubt, be found after each successive reading of this play, but García Gutiérrez had only one tool, his artistry, to bring those elements together; having them come to life on stage, with the right proportion of humor, in a natural situation within the play is what would make a success of such a theatrical creation. Conjectures about this play's being based on a French one are so vague that they can be ignored for lack of evidence. *El caballero de industria,* according to Ferrer del Río (and Guaza quotes him), was one of three plays García Gutiérrez took to Madrid with him, but which was not accepted for performance at the time. After the great success of *El trovador,* however, it was presented and received much praise, being selected for the homage edition.

IV   El caballero leal (*The Loyal Gentleman*)

El caballero leal is a historical drama in three acts, in verse. Published by Repullés in 1841, the edition provides no information about performance. The play occurs in 1055, Spanish era 1093, on September 1. The first two acts take place in the palace of Nájera, court of the King of Navarra, and the third in the Montes de Oca. As it opens, courtiers await the return of King García from his campaign in Aragon, with Catalan and Aragonese soldiers, captives, and a masked warrior whose banner proclaims him to be invincible; he is Fortuño, who is the object of gossip as he enters, challenging anyone who dares speak to his dishonor. He is favored by the King, whom all go to receive. Elvira and Fortuño embrace; he is victorious but will have to leave again for Huarte to observe and ward off the Moors. As the King and his accompaniment arrive, Fortuño and

Elvira mingle with the crowd. Abbot Iñigo of Oña praises the King's victory.

King García detains Elvira, who reminds him that her husband, Fortuño, had a great deal to do with that victory; although he brought her as a lady in waiting for Queen Estefanía, she knows he honors Fortuño because of his interest in Elvira. García recalls their childhood when they loved each other, but he, destined to occupy a throne, had to obey and abide by the tradition and take a royal wife. She also married, perhaps to forget him; she loves García, but also her husband, to whom she will remain loyal. Aznar, who enters on time to hear some of the conversation, implies the obstacle can be removed, since earlier he and Fortuño had quarreled, and are to fight a duel. García admits he thought the Moors would kill Fortuño, but he really seems invincible; sending him to Huarte will be sufficient. Aznar dislikes that decision, since that is his post; García explains he is to keep Fortuño locked up there; the duel can wait.

The second act takes place in Fortuño's house, where Elvira sadly contemplates her husband's armor, together with her servants Gonzalo and Sancha. She is in mourning, and asks Gonzalo if he has summoned Abbot Iñigo and the King. As King García should not be seen entering her house, he will come in by the balcony. The abbot comes and she confesses her troubles; although he says that death freed her from any bond with Fortuño she thinks her inclination for García is a sin. In that case she must repent, the abbot says. She cannot; ten years of fighting her feelings, and the unjust death of Fortuño, are too much to bear; she asks that prayers be said for his eternal rest, for her own peace, and for the assassin. To that effect she offers Don Iñigo some jewels; he says she also should pray, not just buy prayers.

As the abbot leaves, García arrives. Elvira wants to make sure he is not responsible for her husband's death; the King says he was not an accomplice and she makes him swear it. Fortuño's shadow haunts her, and even his armor seems to claim revenge. She prevents García from destroying it and the voice of Fortuño is heard calling Elvira; to their astonishment he climbs the rope ladder, dressed as a villager, and García hides. Elvira believes it is a ghost; he wants to punish her treason, as evidenced by the ladder, but she repeatedly states her innocence. Fortuño sends Elvira to a convent in León and then looks for García, whom he finds. We learn that Moors freed Fortuño, who now wants to be treated as an outsider, serving another king who might wage war on García, since Fortuño himself cannot challenge the King to a duel; the latter replies he can, but Fortuño refuses.

Act three, in a military camp near the Montes de Oca, shows the tent of the King, with courtiers and soldiers who come and go. Some comment on the dissatisfaction and desertion of many knights who disapprove of a war between brothers. Fortuño has joined the enemy, King Ferrando of Castile and León. García and Aznar arrive; the tower of Huarte has to be regained. The King, left to rest, is haunted by a shadow that followed him through the mountains; his Elvira is in a convent; Count Bermudo is dead at his hands; furthermore, García remembers his former attempt to blemish his own mother's honor.[2] Fortuño, in full armor, sits by the sleeping King, telling him he is losing ground among his own, and should learn thereby not to offend his loyal subjects. He cannot kill the defenseless García and wakes him, to the King's surprise, revealing that someone sold the password. García summons Mendo and Garcés to change it, and asks Fortuño to give a new password, being sure that he will use it only to leave the camp safely. However, there is another matter pending, and if he kills him in battle it will be in the line of duty. As Fortuño leaves, the sounds of battle are heard momentarily.

Elvira is brought in, unconscious. Once alone with García he revives her, and she complains of her abduction from the convent, saying she despises him; she once loved him, but he has made it possible for her to hate him. At daybreak the soldiers are ready for battle, as is García, who tells Elvira where to hide to be safe. Abbot Iñigo comes to plead with García to desist from fighting against his own people and his religion. To García's objections that his brother is king of both Castile and Leon, the abbot points out that this apportionment was their father's decision, and that García also has large territories. Mendo brings the sad news that Aznar has been killed by a knight dressed in black, and García leaves in a rage, with his spear ready. Elvira appears and, finding only the abbot, tells him that she was abducted and wants to flee, and then shouts that the King is dead are heard. Fortuño enters, shaken; his duty is to kill Elvira for her treason but she succeeds in convincing him she is innocent, and they embrace. The abbot orders them to kneel as the King is carried by in the background, soldiers dragging their flags are seen, and the sound of sad trumpets is heard; the abbot asks God to have mercy on Fortuño, who covers his face with both hands, as the play ends.

As in other plays based on history, army camps are depicted so as to convey all the impact that suggested military action and necessary equipment can have on stage: armor, spears, shields, trumpets, soldiers coming and going, the mountains in the background, and the sound of battle, as if the author were in the midst of the confrontation. The last scene is especially effective in this respect.

Don García, oldest son of King Sancho of Navarra, a youth in *El Bastardo*, appears here in another period of his life, already a king, but resentful because his father favored his brothers, including the illegitimate Ramiro. His love for Elvira is crucial, since the loyal Fortuño is also loved by her, and she tries to silence her feelings by drowning herself in the love of her husband. It is the reckless behavior of García, moved by an impossible love, even more frustrating because the lady shares his feelings yet will not be disloyal to her husband, that causes the King's downfall. Fortuño is in a peculiar situation; he is loyal to his king, who favors him both because of Elvira and the many virtues he possesses. The death of García in battle against his brother, contrary to his religion and adverse to his subjects, is not as pitiable as the death of some other of the playwright's characters, since García also tried to eliminate Fortuño. The frustration of García overshadows the more or less historic elements of the play; also outstanding are the loyalty of Fortuño and the honorable behavior of Elvira. Enrique López Funes considers this play to be one of transition between a period of creations containing nebulous characters, immoral traits, and tragic and unsavory endings, to the grandiose creation of *Simón Bocanegra*, the beauty of *Venganza catalana* (Catalan Revenge), and the summit of *Juan Lorenzo*.

V Zaida

Zaida, a four-act verse drama (published by Repullés in 1841, with no information concerning performance), takes place in Toledo, shortly after its conquest by King Alfonso VI. In Zaida's house Azamor, a fifteen-year-old slave, admits a gentleman, believing him to be Don Juan, but it is Don Vela, whom Azamor did not recognize since it is night. Vela declares his love to Zaida, who rejects him and tries to send him out, but another caller arrives and Don Vela is hidden. The new arrival is King Alfonso, whom Zaida knows as Don Juan. She loves him but will only agree to marriage. Azamor tells Alfonso privately he has a rival who has fled. The King rushes to the street after him, and the noise of a fight is heard. Benamet, Zaida's father, enters through the balcony with harsh words for her. She invokes her loneliness and the mystery of her mother, who died at her birth and whose name she does not know. Benamet says they will leave Toledo the next day. Azamor offers to find Zaida's suitor and alert him, but a dead man has been found in the street and an angry crowd enters the house by force.

Act two opens in the royal palace of Toledo as King Alfonso tells Don Vela how a young man challenged him on his way out of Zaida's house, and he left him for dead, a revelation in which Vela is most interested. It is suggested that the King (whom Zaida knows as a captain) is willing to share his throne with a Moorish woman, to which end he wants Vela's help. Pero Ansúrez comes in, demanding justice for his murdered son; an old man and his daughter are imprisoned for the crime, but nobody really knows who the aggressor was. The King recognizes the situation and reveals that he is the killer. Ansúrez reminds him of his loyalty and help in crucial times, but Alfonso replies that if Ansúrez does not consider himself his vassal, he can go away. The old man is hurt, and with Doña Jimena swears revenge. She is angry because the King wants to give the throne of Castile to another woman, to Jimena's shame and dishonor. Azamor, who comes to see the King, is surprised to learn he is Don Juan. The latter states he wanted Zaida's love as a man, not as a King. Zaida, freed, refuses to become a queen, because she is of humble origin; later she reconsiders, finding the idea of wearing a crown most appealing. Crying that "Castile has a queen," Jimena asks Zaida when this was not so. In their confrontation, however, it becomes clear that Jimena is not married to Alfonso.

In act three Zaida mourns in her regal chambers; she has lost the love of her father. Alfonso urges her to accompany him to the royal palace, but she knows she is disliked and fears for him. He is about to leave for Portugal; Jimena will enter a convent, but until his return is to be imprisoned in a tower to ensure that she will not harm Zaida. The latter asks his lenience with Jimena, and, when she is brought in, Zaida forgives her conspiracy against her. Jimena resents being subject to so much humiliation. Benamet, asking to speak to Zaida alone, tells her that he was once king of Sevilla, and that her mother was a Christian captive. When Zaida was three years old, he discovered a plan of her mother to flee with another captive who loved her, but Benamet had the man killed and Zaida's mother thrown into the river. Zaida was baptized and her Christian name is Isabel. Alfonso interrupts and Benamet reveals his identity and how he endeavored to conquer more of Spain with the aid of a powerful African king, who instead proclaimed himself king of Andalusia. Alfonso orders his troops to go to Sevilla, not Extremadura.

In the fourth act, at dusk, in the royal palace in Toledo, Zaida awaits Alfonso's return. He has been defeated; Benament is dead. Jimena enters, to the amazement of Alfonso, who left her imprisoned. She wants to legalize her situation and then he can disown her, but with her honor restored; God has punished him for engaging in a war against his own people, many of whom are on her side. The King refuses to marry Jimena, while the roar of people is heard drawing closer. A fearful Zaida listens as Pedro Ansúrez offers to save her, and she will be proclaimed queen. She discloses that she is Christian and tells him her story, which Ansúrez interrupts, explaining that he is her father, not Benamet. Zaida puts on her crown and sits on a chair as various courtiers, Jimena, and Alfonso enter. Isabel (as she is called now) is the queen, and the rebels are to be set free, but Jimena should pay for her treason; however, Zaida forgives her also.

Loosely based on the life of King Alfonso VI and his many women, the play abounds in elements that do not convince us that Zaida deserves all the honor conferred on her, with Jimena pushed aside. The King goes to the aid of the Moorish invaders of the peninsula, so they can acquire more territory, which makes no sense at all. As in other García Gutiérrez plays, a servant is placed in the capacity of defender, counselor, and overall judicious commentator; this time it is Azamor, a Moorish slave only fifteen years old, who utters the most judicious, daring and righteous sentences of the play. This is not verisimilar, both because of his social condition and his youth. The efforts to make Zaida seem so innocent and good, plus hinting at her Christianity, preclude her discovery that she is indeed the daughter of captives of Benamet. Pero Ansúrez's secret is too conveniently brought to light and too readily believed by those who want it to be the truth. Jimena is depicted as scornful because the King disposes of her in favor of a Moorish woman; her clamoring for justice and honor (which she remembered a bit late) do not make her hateful, however; she should be forgiven, indeed, since that is the only thing she achieves in the end.

According to historic accounts, both Jimena and Zaida were concubines of Alfonso VI at different times while he was widowed by one of his five legitimate wives. For that reason Jimena's son and daughter were termed "natural" and not "bastard." Their illicit alliance was ended by a papal order, and Alfonso then married his third wife. Zaida was publicly made to appear as his wife to achieve a pact made with her father, king of Sevilla, who endowed Zaida with possessions she in turn offered to Alfonso. It is also stated that Zaida preceded Jimena as concubine, since, although she agreed to become a Christian, she was not a legitimate wife or a queen. There is confusing chronology, however, as some information is given stating both "year" and "era" with a difference of thirty-eight years; this refers to the Christian era as well as the Spanish (or Caesar's) era, which began thirty-eight years earlier than the Christian. Thus we find year 1100 and era 1138, or year 1126 and era 1164, and the like, in some quotations and documents.

Fr. Burguera praises *Zaida* both as theater and literature, comparing the verses of García Gutiérrez to a river of pearls, but he deplores the historical immorality which is given a coat of decency in the play.[3] Enrique López Funes places *Zaida* in the same transitional period as *El caballero leal*, while José Lomba y Pedraja merely indicates it is based to some extent on a historical episode.

VI El premio del vencedor (*The Prize of the Winner*)

El premio del vencedor is a verse drama in three acts (published by Yenes in 1842 with no additional information). Act one opens in a gothic room where the Count of St. Paul tells his niece Clemencia that she must obey her late father's wishes and marry Pedro, illegitimate son of the Count. She points out that Pedro is neither good looking nor perfect, and even though he is the pride of France and the crusaders she does not love him. But if she must marry him, perhaps he will go back to war, and leave her free. At least she will see the court of Burgundy and leave those gray walls of her uncle's feudal castle. Her sister Blanca enters, happy that they will marry;

she is looking forward to her own wedding to the Duke. Clemencia feels an unrest that she thinks must be love, but does not know the identity of a young man she saw from her window two years before; he was not admitted to the castle, although for three months they communicated with their eyes from a distance.

Pedro interrupts the sisters, telling Clemencia his love is not refined, but strong; he cannot offer her tenderness. Either she accepts him as he is or her wedding will resemble a funeral.

Gutierre and his servant Girón arrive: the former is Clemencia's knight. Pedro says the lady Gutierre is staring at is his cousin, soon to be his wife. Gutierre says he aided a young man wrestling with an animal, and Pedro rushes out to see about his younger brother. Gutierre tells Clemencia he will never again declare his love by making signals at a distance; she replies that she loves him but is being forced to marry Pedro. Gutierre identifies himself as a nobleman from Jaén, lord of Villa-García, and they agree to try to stop the wedding plans. Pedro returns in time to see Gutierre kiss Clemencia's hand, and given the Count's surprise he says it is a Spanish custom. Pedro warns him he will not allow such customs in France.

Act two takes place in the palace of the Duke of Burgundy, in Santomer, as Pedro tells his father that the Spanish knight is there, and that there is no doubt that Clemencia loves him. The Count does not believe it possible. They discuss the condition of women and how they reflect the honor of their men, so they should be treated kindly, but Pedro knows only brute force and battle, and would like to tame women the same way. Left alone when Duke Filipo comes looking for the girls, Pedro yearns for his mountains. Thinking about Clemencia and her attitude, he muses that he does not love her either, so why is he angry? Gutierre and Girón appear, and Gutierre introduces himself to the Duke, giving an account of the war against the Moors in the Iberian Peninsula. Asked what brings him to France, Gutierre says Pedro is robbing him of his happiness. The Count insinuates he wants to challenge and kill Pedro. Clemencia tries to make peace, but both men refuse to call off the duel. She observes that that is not the way to win her, but Gutierre insists his honor is at stake. Duke Filipo ventures that perhaps Clemencia is being forced to marry Pedro, and that her wishes are not being taken into consideration. She explains how she met Gutierre and asks that the challenge be dropped; she will not give her hand to a killer. Both men insist that they are not cowards and want to fight. As Gutierre wants Clemencia to be the prize of the winner, she is most unhappy.

In act three, at the same location, the Count cautions a confident Pedro about the bravery of the Spaniard. Clemencia offers her hand to Pedro if he will desist, but he wants her to mourn Gutierre's death. Clemencia threatens to refuse to marry him and enter a convent, and pray to God to avenge the blood shed by Pedro. She realizes that he is bent only on showing his valor and probably does not love her, and decides to plead with Gutierre, who invokes the laws of honor and agrees not to try to kill Pedro, but only to defend himself. As the encounter nears, Clemencia prays to God to spare Gutierre. The trumpet sounds and shouts are heard; the Count returns, accusing Clemencia of his loss, and cursing her. The French clamor for the death of the foreigner. Gutierre enters as Clemencia complains that he did not keep his word, to which he says Pedro fell, and as the people reacted wanting to kill Gutierre, Pedro stood up. The latter appears, humbly offering his hand to Gutierre, and asks his father to consent to Clemencia and Gutierre's marriage, which the Count does.

The mastery of García Gutiérrez in this play is in the handling of the conflict among brute force (personified by Pedro), the frailty of Clemencia (confined to the walls of a medieval castle, yet yearning for what lies outside), and the more worldly Gutierre, well traveled, and aware of the importance of personal honor. Clemencia does not understand the laws of honor or why they are imposed, causing unhappiness and risking life. García Gutiérrez could have ended this play in any of the several ways envisioned by Clemencia in her anguish: both men mortally wounded, to her sorrow and the Count's; Pedro killed, thus making it impossible for Gutierre to attain his love, since Clemencia would harbor resentment for his part in the duel as well as for placing his honor before her love; or Gutierre killed, with Clemencia mourning her budding love forever, hating Pedro and having to fight a real battle to avoid marrying him and ultimately enter a convent. Her plea reaches Gutierre, who can only act in a limited way since his life is at stake. García Gutiérrez solves the problem by teaching a lesson to all and making them earn what they receive. By making Pedro so rough and crude, not even feeling love for his cousin, there are no victims. I have been unable to locate critical material concerning this play; the usual sources have ignored it.

VII Simón Bocanegra

Simón Bocanegra is a drama in one prologue and five acts, in verse, published by Yenes in 1843. Nicholson Adams claims that it was first performed January 17, 1843, and Juan Alcina recalls that García Gutiérrez was crowned after one of the performances, shortly before his departure for the New World (due to the spontaneity of the audience's request, a laurel crown from a recent production of *Norma* was used).[4] The action is set in Genoa, 1338, outside the Fiesco palace, before its marble facade and balcony, with a view of the church of St. Laurence, two other houses, and two streets. Paolo and Piettro scheme to obtain the ducal crown for Simón Bocanegra, a pirate, since the masses will follow him. Lorenzino Buchetto, a rich candidate interested only in money, will not do as a ruler; besides, Fiesco and the Grimaldis are on Lorenzino's side. The latter goes to warn Fiesco, who is under great stress when he comes to the door and admits Buchetto, saying, "She is dead."

Simón appears with Rafael, who is instructed to find Paolo. In a monologue Simón speculates on why Paolo wants to see him, and reminisces about his beloved Mariana. Returning, Paolo tells Simón that he has been elected to save Naples. Townspeople gather and Piettro tries to sway them, while Simón enters the church and Paolo remains beneath a lit Madonna by Fiesco's door. Piettro, belittling the nobility, says Mariana has not been seen in three years, because the devil, not Fiesco, lives in that house. Someone hurls a rock at a window, which opens on darkness, with no one in sight. After the group retires toward the church wall, Fiesco and Lorenzino come out of the house with a lantern. The former asks his friend to say nothing and leave him with his grief. Simón, leaving the church, meets Fiesco, who is unfriendly to him, but offers to forgive Simón when the latter produces the daughter that he and Mariana had without benefit of clergy. Simón says that he left her in the care of a woman who had died when he returned from one of his voyages, and that he lost track of the girl. Fiesco then enters the church and Simón enters the palace, where he goes to the balcony, takes the lantern illuminating the Madonna to see inside, and finds Mariana dead. As he voices his grief, people appear in the square, with lights, to acclaim him Dux.

Act one takes place in the Grimaldi palace of Genoa, 1362, at dawn. Julieta takes Gabriel Adorno to see her mistress, Susana, inquiring about his bad mood; Susana also wonders why he has been away, but it is better to see him late than never. Gabriel is secretive about his affairs, and she is jealous. He wants to avenge the death of his father, but she argues he should not risk his life and their happiness. Also, there is a man lurking about the palace whom she does not trust. Piettro announces the imminent visit of the Dux. Gabriel and Fiesco, who now calls himself Andrea, discuss their conspiracy and talk of Susana, who is of humble birth, not a Grimaldi as everyone thinks. Gabriel loves her anyway, and if he survives the conspiracy against Bocanegra, he plans to marry Susana; if Gabriel does not return, Andrea will see that the girl enters a convent. As Andrea is taking the place of Susana's father, he consents to the wedding.

The Dux arrives, asking to see Susana alone; he brings a pardon for her brothers (the Grimaldis) and, before he has a chance to put in a good word for Paolo, Susana tells Bocanegra she loves someone, but is being pestered by another suitor: Paolo. He is disappointed to hear she loves another and plans to abduct Susana. Gabriel, wounded, appears, accusing Bocanegra or his men of taking the girl. Simón frees him in spite of his abusive language, ordering Paolo to produce Susana or he will be made to confess under torture.

In act two Piettro asks Lorenzino to hide Susana on Paolo's behalf. Soon the latter arrives with Simón, who has extracted the truth. Lorenzino is relieved when the Dux, instead of being angry at him for concealing the girl, entrusts her to him, upon learning they are father and daughter. Their secret must be kept until the turmoil is over. Everyone thinks the Dux wants Susana for himself. Lorenzino tells her about the conspiracy. Adorno, bent on avenging his father's death, also suspects Simón's intentions. During the third act, in the palace of the Dux, Paolo and Piettro scheme to have Bocanegra killed by Andrea (Fiesco), who can gain entrance via a secret door. Andrea refuses to be a traitor, although Paolo knows his real identity and also that he is proscribed. As Fiesco leaves at his own risk, Gabriel agrees to dispose of Bocanegra.

Adorno is left alone when Susana enters; he inquires as to the situation, but she will not tell him, asking rather that he hide on the balcony when the Dux arrives. She tells Simón of Gabriel and their love, but he argues that Adorno is a traitor; his father died in battle, and Simón was lenient with the other rebels, so his revenge makes no sense. Susana pleads with him, but he has to think things over and she leaves. Bocanegra falls asleep and Gabriel comes in from the balcony; muttering harsh words, he is about to stab the Dux when Susana returns and stops his hand. As they argue, Simón awakens and eventually reveals that he is Susana's father. Adorno refuses to explain how he managed to enter, but as a crowd is heard outside, he offers to fight for Bocanegra.

In the fourth act Andrea (Fiesco) and Paolo are seen using the secret entrance. The latter wants Susana as a prize if they succeed in overthrowing the Dux; Fiesco is to bring his people and hide them until the signal is given. Simón, Gabriel, Piettro, and several senators and soldiers appear to celebrate their victory. Simón orders his wealth distributed among the wounded and other victims on either side; he is fair in battle and afterwards. Gabriel is praised and will be rewarded. Paolo mentions to Piettro in an aside that there is a certain goblet which only the Dux uses that will be their weapon. Amid talk of a wedding, Paolo tells Fiesco that death is coming to the Dux, so they must flee. Fiesco instructs one of his servants to accompany Paolo to the mountains and, once there, to be merciless with him. . . .When those assembled leave, Simón goes to the balcony, which displays the square full of lights; he reminisces about his crossing the sea and how his ambition had placed him in a high position, but he is unhappy. Fiesco appears and reveals his identity and alludes to the unfinished issue of his pardon, disclosing that Simón is dying. Lights in the square dim as Bocanegra feels the effect of the poison; he collapses on a chair as some men enter bringing Susana. He blesses his daughter and unites her and Gabriel, instructing Fiesco to announce that Gabriel Adorno is the new Dux. The crowd is heard filling the square as Fiesco proclaims the new ruler from the balcony, at the same time that he announces the death of Simón Bocanegra.

The very intricate series of conspiracies make this play (based on the actual, historical life of the pirate Simon Bocanegra)[5] seem a novel taken to the stage. The complex duplicity of some characters is somewhat confusing, especially when coupled with the use of assumed names. Serving two masters for personal gain, greed, love, jealousy, resentment, and the twenty-four-year lapse between the prologue and the first act are among the elements that contribute to the difficulty of following the story. A second reading is helpful in bringing identities into focus and clearing up obscure points; actually, there are no loose ends. Simón Bocanegra emerges as a powerful, feared man, simultaneously respected and maligned, who tempers his anger when forced to fight, is fair to his enemies, and yet is intransigent with treason. He is seen by Fiesco, Susana, and Gabriel Adorno each in a different light according to their personal feelings and circumstances (not always clear to others, since certain secrets must be kept until there is no more unrest). The devious Paolo is not punished on stage. Piettro, Lorenzino, and other characters who function as mere accessories to the main plot are left as they were when the play ends.

A good deal of familiarity with the theater is needed, both as a spectator as well as a participant, to properly imagine this play (as well as others by García Gutiérrez) and to follow the action, closely related to the complex set. The audience or the reader must be alert and ready to discover parts of secrets and intrigues that will be resolved eventually, but which the author will masterfully conceal for a long time. Failure to place on stage certain scenic details or properties specified by the author would harm the continuity as well as clarity of a play so complicated as *Simón Bocanegra*. The set is not merely a backdrop; the church is there for a purpose, as is the light at the door of Fiesco's palace, and the balcony. All are used. The prologue alone brings together enough background information to develop several plays (Father Blanco suggests three, but I had reached that conclusion before reading his book). One could develop the love of Simón and Mariana (Fiesco's daughter) and their separation, with Simón taking their daughter Susana with him. Another play would follow the adventures of the pirate and his involvement in politics, a rough man torn between his life braving the seas and the love of a distant woman, while a third could involve the reaction of Fiesco to his daughter's illicit affair with Bocanegra, the ensuing sequestered life imposed upon Mariana, her hard decision to entrust little Susana to Simón (a buccaneer), the shame and resentment of Fiesco, and the death of Mariana on the same day Bocanegra returns, years later. This prologue is essential to the play, which begins at the moment of Simón's return and Mariana's death earlier that day, and then follows Simón's ascent to power, while his unhappiness increases. Once he finds his daughter Susana his joy does not last, since, after a brief period of happiness, treason, gossip, and resentment lead to his death by poisoning.

Among the critics, López Funes has a great deal of praise for

Simón Bocanegra, which he considers a higher expression of themes of *El rey monge*, admirably constructed, and in which history and legend are embraced by art. Nicholson Adams likes this play also, especially the way it develops, but says not a word about its being based upon a historical figure, and very little about the Verdi opera. Also, in Adams's plot résumé Fiesco is said to aid Paolo in poisoning Simón, when in reality he is opposed. Fr. Blanco García also likes *Simón Bocanegra,* praising the strong scenes and their beauty, one by one, not relating them to the whole. He notes that the prologue alone contains enough material for three more dramas.

VIII Las bodas de Doña Sancha
(The Wedding of Doña Sancha)

An 1843 verse drama in three acts (published the same year by Repullés) offers no information as to performance. The action occurs in León, May 12, 1028, where courtiers await the arrival of Count García of Castile, then thirteen years old, who is to marry Princess Sancha of León, uniting the two kingdoms. To the surprise of many, Pedro Cortacabezas, a known bandit, is in León. Rodrigo and Iñigo, Counts of Vela, plan to stop García but Iñigo feels compassion for the child. Ferran reminds Rodrigo that their father was a traitor who brought the Moors to Castile. Sancha, who is twenty-two years old, tells her beloved Fernando, son of the King of Navarra, that they must forget their love, since she is about to marry, though not by choice. He protests, but duty comes first. García arrives with great accompaniment and Sancha finds him appealing and handsome. He pays her compliments and wants to meet her knights, among whom he discovers the brothers Vela and points them out as traitors. As they protest their innocence García says their actions will prove their repentance. Inasmuch as the young Count will go to Oviedo next morning, the Velas plot their revenge. In the following act, Ferran and Diego keep watch over the palace, pending the departure of García, mistrusting the Velas. Fernando stops Rodrigo from seeing García, and Sancha enters, urging him to leave León so they can have peace. Rodrigo says that his contempt for Count Gonzalo led him to aid the Moors, but he has nothing against García; Sancha believes him. Later, when the young Count asks her if the wedding is to her liking, she assures him it is, but asks that he forgive Rodrigo. García agrees to see him, although he suspects he seeks revenge because his father offended Rodrigo's. Before his courtiers, García puts Rodrigo in charge of Atienza, Nájera, and Peñafiel.

In act three, at night, Jimena agrees to help Fernando see Sancha after García leaves for Oviedo, for which the Princess scolds her. Voices are heard and Rodrigo appears with a drawn sword, seeking refuge. Sancha points to a door in her chambers as men pour in looking for the killer of Count García. Sancha, horrified, asks to see the dead young man, and he is brought in on a stretcher. She bemoans the crime, offering her hand to whoever brings the assassin to her if he is noble, or riches as a reward if he is not, then instructs the men to place García in another room. When she is alone, Rodrigo comes out of hiding and she makes him confess his crime. He gives as a reason the fact that he loves her. Sancha leaves and Rodrigo tries to escape, but Fernando stops him; after a violent exchange of words, they draw their swords and Rodrigo dies in the fight. Sancha will marry Fernando, but only when the events of that night are no longer recent. Various aspects of this play are based on the historical episode of Count García, who was assassinated by the Counts of Vela. Again there is no critical material concerning this play, although the question of historicity versus invention offers an obvious area for investigation.

IX De un apuro otro mayor (*From Trouble a Bigger One*)

A verse comedy in two acts, performed in the Cruz Theater in March 1843 as a benefit for the actress Bárbara Lamadrid, this play was published by Repullés the same year.[6] At midnight, April 23, 1521, the first act begins in Zamora as Don Diego, the Governor, impatiently calls Don Blas de Hinestrosa and asks him to send a note to the Duke of Haro to the effect that the city is safe in his hands. Now the queen and the cardinal will not subject him to ridicule; he is not afraid of the *comuneros*, since Padilla has been caught. Mendo, a servant, announces Inés, who is looking for her brother Diego, but instead finds only Blas, whom she considers a bit stupid (he believes she returns his love). Mendo secretly gives the lady a letter from Don Juan de Herrera, who is in Zamora and in danger. Mendo will be her ally. Don Juan enters, wrapped in his cape, having escaped from Villalar; wounded and defeated, he must find refuge in Portugal. It is implied that he and Inés are secretly married. As another gentleman arrives, Mendo is surprised to see Juan hiding in Inés's room.[7] Don Fernando, whom Inés obviously does not wish to see, had come to see Diego, and now wants to visit her; his faction was victorious in Villalar, and now he pursues a fugitive he followed there. Inés is very nervous and can barely hide what Fernando suspects; he offers to trade the outlawed man for her love, at which she is horrified. When Diego comes, Fernando tells him that a rebel is in his house. Diego dislikes the spy, but knows that his life is at stake if he displeases the king. Juan reveals himself and Diego orders Blas to keep him in custody. Inés decides she must talk to Blas.

In act two, in the same room, Blas, hoping to see Inés, finds Mendo instead. Both know about Villalar, and Mendo learns that one of the fugitives is prisoner in the house. Blas hopes to bend Inés to his wishes, convinced she loves him, but soon learns otherwise, and fears for his life. Inés promises to take all responsibility for whatever happens, and Juan, sad but resigned to his lot, is allowed to see her. Diego is heard inside and Inés cautions Juan not to try to escape since there are guards posted everywhere, so he returns to his confinement. The Governor completes some papers to be sent with Blas to the Portuguese border to stop would-be refugees. Inés plans to replace the messenger, and tells Blas that his own death sentence is also in those papers. Gullible Blas believes her, even her statement that there is a rumor that he started a rebellion against Diego. Blas concludes that someone must have been using his name; Inés keeps the papers, but Blas tells Diego he is innocent. Exasperated, Diego learns from Blas that Inés told him about the conspiracy. When Diego sends Blas out, Inés pleads for Juan, appealing to his brotherly love. Diego insists upon his duty, and Inés reveals that Juan has fled to Portugal, thanks to her scheme. Diego considers Juan a rebel; she explains that they were married secretly by a priest; she is willing to give her life for Juan's freedom. Diego believes the cardinal will be inflexible. As for Fernando, Inés says he wanted her love, and then confesses she used Blas. The Governor forgives the latter, but says Inés should leave. Fernando accuses Diego of treason; he knows Juan is safe in Portugal and will keep the secret if he is given Inés, otherwise he will tell the cardinal. The Governor challenges Fernando, who falls during the ensuing duel as Inés and Blas knock on the door. Diego sends his sister to Portugal and tells Blas he is to accompany her; pointing to the door he says that the mortally wounded man is the escaped prisoner. Blas is confused, but he is not about to receive any more explanations. Diego asks Inés to think well of him, to say to Juan he regrets having lost his friendship, but that if he returns to Zamora, Diego must take his life.

Blas, portrayed as not too bright, sees things in a fog that distorts their true meaning, and is easily swayed by the words of Inés, which he interprets in the light of her imaginary love for him. Not intelligent enough to test the veracity of her assertions, he reveals the source of the supposed intrigue to the one person who should not know: Don Diego. The latter, the Governor, is torn between his responsibilities and feelings for his sister, whom he allows to achieve happiness when he could be cruel, since in the name of the high post he occupies and the honor that goes with it, as well as for personal reasons, he could punish her. Mendo, *gracioso* in his condition as servant, is not against asking for a reward in exchange for a favor, doing an errand, or keeping a secret. His speech is crisp and humorous. I found no reviews or other critical commentary relevant to this play.

X Gabriel

Gabriel, a verse drama in three acts, published by Repullés in 1844, lacks performance information. As the action commences in Barcelona we learn that Inés loves Juan (whom she knows as Félix) but she will not hurt Jaime, the older gentleman in whose house she lives. Jaime wants to know how Félix stands on politics, suspecting that he is a traitor. Gabriel (unidentified, seemingly living in the same house as Jaime and Inés) announces the visit of a veiled lady who wants to see Jaime in private. She is Elena, an unexpected reminder of the past. They recall their love, the illegitimate daughter they had, and the curse of an old man. Elena, who has a suitor, nonetheless wants to marry Jaime, to his great surprise. She suspects that the woman who lives with him is a rival, while he insists no woman is hiding behind that door; it is Félix. She recognizes him as Juan de Cardona, who is not happy to see her there. Engaged to Elena, he pursues Inés; among his competitors may be Jaime, who raised her, and another unnamed, rugged Catalan. Juan wants to abduct Inés, but Jaime may have to be confined so he can carry out his plan.[8]

In the second act Inés awaits news of Jaime and the verdict on whether he is a traitor. Gabriel tells her that he harbors a hopeless love, but she considers him a brother and does not realize that he loves her. Juan arrives with good news about Jaime and hints that Inés loves him. She insists that it is not so, but that she cannot hurt him. Juan proves not so tender and idealistic as she thought; horrified, she realizes that he is calculating and cold, and wants only to be her lover. Gabriel comes between them and defends Inés. To avoid a duel, Inés agrees to leave with Juan, but Gabriel says she may go only as a wife. Juan says Gabriel cannot give her hand to him, demonstrating his dishonorable intentions, so Juan/Félix is sent away. Elena and Jaime arrive; the latter now knows Félix is a spy whom he had trusted, and who accused him of treason—a true allegation. As Juan leaves, Jaime awaits the signal from the rebels. Gabriel and Inés join Jaime and Elena with mixed emotions, as fires are ignited all over Barcelona, indicating that the insurrection has begun.

Act three finds Jaime asleep in his bedroom, adjoining Gabriel's, on a divided stage. Gabriel wants to talk to Jaime before they leave, since the older man looked after him and Inés, whom he loves. Jaime confesses that as a young man he went to Madrid and, to improve his status, changed his name and pretended to be a count. With dishonest monetary deals he broke into the court's social sphere, falling in love with a noblewoman who returned his feelings. Inés, born as a result, is not aware who her parents are; she also has a fortune which Jaime has made for her. Confused, Gabriel stops Jaime from leaving and facing his treason; the young man wants to depart alone.

With Jaime asleep, Inés comes to see him and speaks of sacrificing her life to him in gratitude. Juan surprises her and she refuses to go off with him. He explains that his house and family were ransacked, reveals his real name and adds that he is loyal to the new king. Her love rekindled, she decides to leave with Juan, who in an aside says he has taken revenge on Jaime. Gabriel, ready to leave, sees them and alerts Jaime; Elena enters, and says that the other woman will not come back. After a heated discussion, Jaime tells Elena that Inés is their daughter, not a rival. Each blaming the other, both try to go after her, but Gabriel returns with Inés, who has fainted. She must not know he killed Juan. When she recovers, Inés says she now knows who she is, so her error was even greater. It is time to set things straight, but Gabriel is going to war. If, when he returns, Inés is cured of her love, she will marry him.

Not a happy tale, with undercover activities, conspiracy, jealousy, treason, and mystery, the plot line is very difficult from the beginning, since it takes a long time to identify the characters in their interrelationships as well as in their intentions. Their feelings of love are heavily influenced by those of duty or what they believe to be their proper behavior or indebtedness, not helped along in their groping by those in a position to clear up matters. Elena, Jaime, and Juan have a dubious past and present due to different causes, while Gabriel and Inés exercise the loyalty they owe to a man who, under unexplained circumstances, took charge of them. The outcome of the play, therefore, is logical, considering the nebulous atmosphere in which all has taken place. A sudden change of heart on the part of Inés would have been too much to ask the audience to believe, because the revelation of her true relationship with Jaime, her rival, Elena, and the duplicity and death of her beloved Félix (Juan), even more dear to her when he tells her his real name and background, are too many emotions to handle at one time and then resolve in a few seconds in order to suddenly love Gabriel. The two consistent and innocent characters see it that way and act accordingly. The reader, however, as well as the audience, suffer prolonged confusion before being able to follow the intricacies of the plot. Lomba y Pedraja, in the one critical reference located, notes that the intrigue is so absorbing that it overshadows any other considerations about this play.

XI Empeños de una venganza (*The Pledges of a Vengeance*)

Empeños de una venganza, a three-act verse drama printed by Repullés in 1844, also lacks information about performance. It is set during the reign of King Felipe III (1598–1621). Diego, calling Fortún "Aben-Zaide," gives him a paper he accepts gladly. The latter calls Diego "Almanzor" and cautions him to be careful going into town. Diego hopes to avert trouble by pretending to give his daughter Isabel to a gentleman protégé of the King. Only Hernando knows this, and he does not trust the Moor. Diego tells Hernando to try to ascertain via Beatriz, a trusted maid and confidant of his wife Leonor, why she is always sad, using as a pretext the impending wedding of their daughter. Isabel (as well as her mother, Leonor, and Beatriz) dislikes the intended bridegroom, Don Juan. The confidant Beatriz knows that Leonor bemoans the death, years before, of Félix, in the Gulf of Mexico, although he had married another woman by then. Fernando, posing as Félix, wrapped in a cape, wants to see Isabel, and tells Beatriz that he was saved when Félix drowned. Beatriz hides him as the ladies approach. Isabel is crying; she loves Carlos. Fernando makes his presence known to Leonor when the girl leaves, and reveals it was he who saved her from a fire in Burgos years before, under the name of Carlos. When Leonor scolds him, he says she was unfaithful, the reason for which Félix left. (There is mystery in all this not revealed to us at the moment.) Fernando alleges he has Félix's papers, and also knows that her husband, Diego, conspires against the King. Leonor had written Félix inquiring about their son, whose parents denied him his name, and the letters are now in Fernando's hands; either Isabel marries him or he will tell Diego the whole story.

In act two Fernando asks Fortún, one of his servants, about Diego, who has been imprisoned for conspiracy, and Isabel is angry at Fernando's tactics. Juan comes against Fernando, but Isabel stops both men, who will fight a duel that night. Fernando prepares some of his men to overpower Juan if he is wounded. Leonor tells Hernando to dispose of her fortune to save her husband. Later she overhears Juan and Fortún talking and is surprised to learn that the latter is in the service of Fernando. Juan's supposed mother, on her death bed, confided to Fortún that Juan was not her son; Fortún has documents and a portrait to prove who is the real mother. Juan urges Fortún to bring him the papers that night, and Leonor rejoices.

Act three takes place at night, in a garden. Diego, now free, is ready to take revenge, to which Hernando says that Leonor is responsible for his freedom. Fortún, in the dark, mistakes Diego for Juan and gives him the papers. Rushing off as Fernando is coming, when the moon illuminates the garden, Diego sees the portrait: Leonor is Juan's mother. Fernando, his servant Nuño and other men come seeking Juan, but instead find Leonor, who was going to meet Diego. As they search the garden for a man they saw crossing, Leonor pretends that Fernando, who once was her lover, still is. Diego appears, and Fernando is determined to kill him; he calls his men and Leonor tries to stop the trouble. The appearance of Juan and Fortún adds to the confusion, with Juan wanting to recover the documents, the others fighting, and Fernando shouting he is about to die. Isabel arrives and Diego, mortally wounded, reveals that Juan is Isabel's half brother; Fernando had taken the identity of Félix. Diego forgives everyone and dies.

The first part, when Moorish names are used, is not followed by a resolution of the apparent treason, which subsequently takes second place to the honor and love intrigue, brought to a head by the evil intentions of Fernando, serving to set matters straight as far as Leonor, Isabel and Juan are concerned. The reading of this play and its performance (the end for which it was written) vary to the point that the live action will be superior to the written word as the play unfolds, as happens with *Simón Bocanegra* and other complicated García Gutiérrez plays.

XII La mujer valerosa (*The Brave Woman*)

La mujer valerosa, a verse drama in four acts, published in Mérida de Yucatán by Castillo and Co., 1844, is dedicated to Doña Manuela Escudero de Domínguez. The play is set in Toledo, during the popular revolutionary uprising of the *comuneros* of Castile. Inés and her brother Tello are torn by her love for Pedro, a captain not to be trusted even by his closest friends. A very complicated story, the love conflict is pitched against assorted acts of treason and heroism instigated mainly by María Pacheco, wife of Juan Padilla, one of the *comunero* leaders who, with the others, was executed at Villalar. His death only makes his wife more willing than ever to fight, in part because she feels responsible for having incited him to undertake the rebellion. Victim of a conspiracy, betrayed and defeated, as were the *comuneros* and their followers, she is exiled to Portugal. Maria exhorts her allies to fight for exiled Spain; she, outlawed, will pray for her country.

This is another García Gutiérrez play inspired by Spanish epics or portions thereof, this one dealing with the uprising of the *Comuneros de Castilla* (1520) against Charles V (I of Spain), whose court was overflowing with trusted Flemish courtiers, intent not on preserving the newly inherited Spanish empire, but on living off it. As in *El Encubierto de Valencia*, *Venganza catalana*, and *Juan Lorenzo*, the author was interested in the lot of the common people, exploited, denied justice, and at the mercy of those in power, without a voice in their own destiny.

María Pacheco, according to history, received the news of her husband's death in her oratory; she then organized the resistance of Toledo, but eventually had to surrender. After a time, when a compromise was reached and the siege lifted, she was exiled. Years later the king declared an amnesty, excluding Juan Padilla, "executed," and his wife. Even after her death, a request was denied for her to repose in Villalar next to her husband. My search revealed no criticism of this play.

XIII El secreto del ahorcado (*The Secret of the Hung Man*)

El secreto del ahorcado is a verse drama in four acts, the second part of *Los alcaldes de Valladolid* (The Mayors of Valladolid, 1844), which I have been unable to find. This sequel, written in 1845, was published in Mérida de Yucatán in 1846 by Castillo and Co., and is dedicated to Don Miguel Barbachano and General Francisco Peraza. The action takes place in Mérida, Mexico, in May 1704.

In the first act Captain Argaiz tries several times to see Honoria, always crying. Juana, her maid, wrings from him the fact that he loves Honoria, but understands that the loss of Fernando is too much for her. Justice will be done to those who desecrated the house of God by spilling blood upon the altar. Honoria, rejecting Argaiz's words of love, decides to see the governor; meanwhile Fray José, a Franciscan monk, comes with Doña Juana Bolio to appeal to Honoria. They hide when she returns to her house with Álvaro Rivaguda, the governor, who assures her that Ayuso and Tovar are as good as dead. When he leaves, Doña Juana reveals her presence and pleads with Honoria. Startled, the latter asks Doña Juana how she would feel if her husband and son were assassinated, and her pleas were mocked. Juana leaves in despair and Honoria orders the house locked, but Ayuso, wrapped in his cape, manages to enter. Amazed to see him free, and angry, she reminds him of his crime. He insists he was deceived and Don Martín is to blame, stating he has proof that Don Fernando and Honoria's brother were killed under his orders. Ayuso then tries treacherously to kill Honoria who faints after calling for help. Argaiz enters after soldiers take Ayuso. Act two opens in the Mérida jail, where Don Alvaro Rivaguda dictates orders to prosecute anyone who tries to free the prisoner. Fray José comes to tell Alvaro, in secret, that the condemned men must be freed, because Doña Juana Bolio wishes it (she is very religious). The governor refuses and the friar implies that he, Fray José, may have facilitated their escape the night before. Honoria attempts to see the governor but Doña Juana is with him, implying there may be another guilty party not in jail, so the execution should be postponed; Ayuso has proof in some letters he keeps with him at all times. Rivaguda agrees to the deal and, once alone, orders Ayuso brought in in secret. However, Honoria and Argaiz listen from concealment, and when the governor tries to take the letters from the prisoner, Honoria interrupts. Ayuso is sent back to his cell.

In the third act Honoria shows remorse as the men have been executed. Her maid reminds her that is what she wanted, and says to forget and pay attention to Argaiz, who loves her. Fray José inquires whether, now that Honoria has had her revenge, she would pardon an accomplice if there were one; he tries to elicit the name from her, suspecting it is Don Martin, Juana Bolio's husband. Honoria wants the score settled and also she wants Juana to wonder if the tomb guarded her secret, as she wishes to humble her. Captain Argaiz will get her the proof. As a choir of monks sings in the background, Honoria prays for the souls of the men executed. In the last act, which shows a street where Honoria lives, and the cathedral across from her house, a comedy of errors is played out, as Argaiz goes into the crypt; Fray José, hoping to obtain a high religious post, aids the governor. All of these and Doña Juana try to retrieve from Ayuso's corpse the incriminating papers. After many surprises and scary situations bring all the characters to the scene, a bitter exchange between Honoria and Doña Juana takes place. Honoria, first humiliating the other lady, destroys the letters retrieved by Argaiz; after much forgiving of one another, Doña Juana and the governor will be matron of honor and best man at Honoria and Argaiz's wedding.

This is a play that lends itself to very effective staging; it is secretive, full of shadows and dim lights. It would be more complete and comprehensible if the first part were available, since it is not clearly explained what the crime was, how it came about, or how Don Martín was implicated. Also there is a question as to what relationship the victims had with Honoria, since at times they seem to be her husband and at others her father and brother. As is the case with García Gutiérrez's other plays published in Mexico, there are no available reviews or other relevant critical information on this drama.

XIV   Los hijos del tío Tronera
(The Children of Uncle Tronera)

Los hijos del tío Tronera is a one-act parody *of El trovador*, in verse, printed by Lalama in 1850. Performed for the first time in 1849 in the Comedia Theater, it takes place in the main square of Dos Hermanas, a village near Sevilla, showing the jail on one side and a house with windows on the other. Inés comments with her friend Rita upon how she wept when Manuel, her boyfriend, went to jail. Later he escaped and found her talking with Bartolo, the Mayor, on the stairway of her house; Manuel was quite angry. He is seen coming and Rita leaves. Inés explains to the young man that she thought it was he singing under her window, so she came down, to find instead that it was the Mayor; then Manuel showed up and hit him. When Bartolo arrives, Inés takes shelter in her house. The men argue, drawing their knives, but since one of them is a fugitive, and the other the Mayor, they agree to go outside the town's limits to vent their anger.

Curra, a gypsy, and Meco discuss Manuel and philosophize on a folksy level about crime and punishment. Manuel is said to be nice and cheery, and he sings better than anyone else. Curra recalls how her mother was sent to prison, reflecting she had little luck, and her descendants none; however, Manuel is not her son—she only raised him. He arrives asking about the song she was singing. Curra tells him she once had a mother (Manuel is glad to hear that)[9] who stole something from Tronera, Bartolo the Mayor's father, who had her imprisoned; her poor health and too much work finished her, but not before she made Curra promise she would do something big to Tronera. Curra, though in tears, stole his child, drowning her sorrow in *manzanilla* (a strong dry white wine). Her remorse was such that she took the child and put him in the turnstyle of a convent, but once back home Troneriya (little Tronera) was there: under the influence of the *manzanilla* she had put her own child in the orphanage. Manuel then says he is not her son, but she insists he is, demanding that he avenge her mother, to which he agrees because, after all, Curra supports him.

Bartolo fled; it is almost daybreak, and if Inés agrees to go off with Manuel to Sevilla he will put everything at her feet, except riches. Meco readies the horse, wondering how to alert Inés. Singing is the answer, but Meco is hoarse, so Manuel must sing. After much arguing, Inés comes down. Manuel tells her he dreamed they were by the river; the moon was like a cheese, and there appeared a witch on a broomstick, screeching to him to go away. A great thunderstorm shook everything and suddenly Inés was a mound of bones; then he saw the jug of branch water from which he had been drinking, and became calm. And for that he goes away? inquires Inés. Yes, he is a fugitive. She invokes her honor and they argue, with Manuel suggesting, "Don't come with me, I will take you away if you faint and blame me." She obeys, but Meco rushes there with the news that Curra is being pursued by the authorities, and Manuel goes to help her. When Bartolo and a guard arrive, Inés learns that the gypsy and Manuel have been caught, and she pleads with the Mayor to free them. Bartolo refuses, as Manuel loves her but Inés replies that he is always in trouble, not a good risk for a husband. Bartolo agrees, if Inés pays heed to him, to free Manuel on condition that the latter leave town in three minutes.

In jail, meanwhile, as Manuel tries to lull Curra to sleep, Inés enters, informing him he is free, but he doubts her; also, what about Curra? Inés tells Manuel that she has taken poison,[10] to which Manuel reacts by saying that was stupid.[11] She dies, and he is sorry it happened that way. Bartolo arrives, and in his disappointment tells Carranza to hit Manuel when he leaves the jail. He leaves, having forgotten Curra, and a scream is heard. The gypsy awakens, inquires about her son, hears his cry, and tells Bartolo that she stole Manuel from Tronera, so he was his brother. Bartolo strikes the gypsy, cursing her, as Curra falls, saying, "Mother, I have avenged you."

The beginning is done so much in jest that it is difficult to imagine García Gutiérrez was really intent on writing a parody of such a tragic play as *El trovador*. The language is festive, natural, appropriate to the Andalusian people (the author was from Cádiz); he achieves double meaning by the use of a word here and there, so much on target that what could become a broad farce falls short of being so just in time. After the initial problem is established, and some elements of the play being parodied are identified, the mood changes somewhat as the reader or audience recognizes more of the dramatic scenes and plot, and is prevented from laughing by remembrance of the tragedy. The basic story is then brought down to the level of ordinary people in a small town. The girl Inés is of no particular social class; Bartolo as Mayor is able to wield some power, but only insofar as maintaining justice is concerned. Manuel, a winsome young man, but a loser, is always in trouble with the law, and a fugitive because he fled from jail. None of the noble enterprises of the original drama reappears here; even the sacrifice of Inés is dealt with in a casual and primitive manner, as is her concern for her honor; it is the thing to do, but her pure feelings are shown by her unappreciated actions. She is willing to go off with Manuel only if it is done in such a way that she can keep her good name. Bartolo is not appealing to her, so for that reason she will die before being his and untrue to herself and the man she loves. The gypsy is also simplified in her thoughts and feelings; the ordeal of her mother and subsequent actions to avenge her are also toned down. In keeping with the low social class of the people involved (that is, not of noble origin), the death of Manuel is unexpected since he is struck down as an escaping prisoner, as Bartolo ordered.

The amusing dialogue of the first part has given way to the needless tragedy of the ending without losing the steady tone of the story. The uncomplicated speech of the characters constantly evokes their status and their problems, as the reality of their daily lives is a more tangible element than their feelings, which have to take second place because their life is not so idle or so easy that they can dwell on them. Here García Gutiérrez shows once more his versatility, his exact measure, his ability to write humorously within a serious framework, as opposed to the gloomy atmosphere omnipresent in *El trovador,* although it seems almost sacrilegious to poke fun at such a tragic piece.

Nicholson Adams is of the opinion that this parody was a way for García Gutiérrez to poke fun at Romanticism, calling his own play "una tontería" (silly), without consequence. Adams then gives a list of some other writers who also wrote parodies, but of García Gutiérrez he stipulates that his is a penetrating satire and not just an exercise.

CHAPTER 5

Plays from 1850 to 1870

I Plays of the 1850s

AFECTOS *de odio y amor* (Feelings of Hate and Love) is a verse comedy in three acts published by Domínguez in 1850. Performed at the Comedia Theater (no date given), it takes place in Evora, Portugal, in 1580. Inés inquires as to why Teodora, who lives in the same house since she is alone in the world, is so sad. Both girls love a captain by the name of Juan, unaware that it is the same man. Diego, Inés's father, wants Teodora to marry a German by the name of Aremberg, but she dislikes him as much as his nationality. She suspects Spanish soldiers killed her mother, but one of them saved her. Diego makes Aremberg believe Teodora loves him in order to keep him on his side, and has him hide when Pereira brings news of the advancing Spaniards (Pereira distrusts the Germans). Juan turns out to be the soldier who saved Teodora; they recognized each other as he is lodged in Diego's house. He confesses his love for Teodora, which she does not reject. Diego is forced to lodge the Spanish captain, whose men are housed elsewhere in Evora, and he wastes no time in alerting the Germans.

In the second act Inés and Teodora realize they love the same man, but as Inés assumes that she is the one elected by Juan, they plan to test him. While dressing he confides to his aide, Girón, that he loves Teodora. In conversation with Diego, the Spanish Captain is put on guard, as he suspects the old man to be devious. Aremberg arrives with a letter for Don Juan, which contains a chain and a crucifix. Beatriz, a curious maid, leads Teodora to examine Juan's effects to see if they reveal anything about a lady. Instead they find the crucifix, which belonged to Teodora's mother, so she concludes that he must have been the assassin. Enraged, she promises Diego she will give her hand to Aremberg, and then confronts Juan with the evidence. He proves he not only saved her mother, but that she was the one who sent him the chain, crucifix, and letter. Seeking revenge, Teodora realizes that Aremberg is a traitor and warns Juan to flee, but he is made a prisoner in the house. Inés, who still believes Aremberg and Teodora will marry, no longer considers the latter a rival.

In act three, in Juan's room, Girón laments his lot hoping that Don Lope de Figueroa will come soon and save them. Such things happen in times of war, comments Juan. Teodora sends food, arms, and a letter: Aremberg has fled and Diego's scheme is collapsing. The two girls visit Juan and Inés tests his love; he says his feeling for Teodora is fictional. Pretending they are also prisoners he hides them when Diego enters. The latter tries to win Juan over to his cause, and when the captain refuses to do so, Diego accuses him of a crime which Juan proves he did not commit. The real enemy of Teodora's mother turns out to have been Diego, who sacked the widow's house to retrieve papers proving his debts to her dead husband. Teodora hears this, but Inés is too far away. Diego then attacks Juan, who defends himself with a pistol as Girón comes to his aid. The women come out of hiding and place themselves between them; Juan dons Diego's cape and leaves, as soldiers arrive seeking him. The town is bubbling with excitement at the arrival of Lope de Figueroa, and Diego confesses his guilt. Juan tells the crowd the old man is not a traitor, and Teodora forgives him. Juan will ask for Teodora's hand in marriage. Although no comments are found concerning this play, it was among those included in the homage volume of García Gutiérrez's selected works, suggesting a degree of esteem on the part of the editors.

Los millonarios (The Millionaires) is another three-act verse comedy published in 1851 by González, lacking data as to performance. Set in Villaviciosa de Odón, the action commences in Rufo's house as his daughters Adela and Rosa embroider while Facundo enjoys the scene. Adela cautions him not to flatter Rosa so much, but he does so repeatedly. Rosa, who plans to become a nun, is nonetheless happy about Facundo's words. Luisito, a rival, loves both girls. Facundo complains that Adela is impossible and jealous, affirming he loves Rosa, whom the maid Pepa terms "the millionaire." When Ramón and Luisito inquire what Facundo is doing there, Pepa explains he is a friend of the master of the house, who comes and goes at will. Rufo joins them and they remark about Facundo's always being there. Ramón is furious because he also is after the millionaire, but Rufo defends his friend. An agitated Mamerto reports to Rufo in private that he witnessed a brawl in a bar and that the authorities are looking for one Eusebio Andrade, but Rufo leaves Mamerto talking.[1] When Facundo happens by, Mamerto observes he fits the description of the wanted man, a coincidence which is denied. Once alone, however, Facundo wonders if someone betrayed him, for he is in fact Eusebio Andrade. A letter for him arrives which Adela attempts to see, suspecting it is from another woman. Facundo refuses, again criticizing her as jealous and ill-tempered.

In act two Facundo looks for Rosa, and while he awaits her he answers the letter he received, which he reads aloud. It is from Pantoja, who is in jail: Facundo must help him or Pantoja will implicate him. When Rosa comes, Facundo declares his love for her. Luis surprises them in the middle of the conversation, deciding to begin an intrigue with Adela. Facundo hints to his friend that Luisito is a Don Juan and Rufo should be more careful with his daughters. Rufo reveals that Rosa is the child of his second marriage, and that her uncle Gregorio has left her a fortune. Facundo, interested, inquires if there is not another possible heir. Quarreling with Adela, Facundo returns her letters; she discovers one extra and believes it is the one she wanted to see. Actually, it is a fake, twisting Pantoja's words, with a forged signature; Facundo returns, feigning concern, to retrieve it.

Rufo asks Facundo at the beginning of the last act why he did not confide his problems, and offers him money. Facundo, pretending pride, accepts it but offers a receipt. He despises Adela for triggering this situation: he is not about to lose a million. Pepa brings Rufo a letter from Lima, and meanwhile Facundo tells Rosa that she is wealthy but he is not, so her father will not allow the match. She will not renounce her money, and hesitates about eloping, but finally agrees. Rufo learns from the letter that Uncle Gregorio in fact left seven assorted heirs, and more frauds and debts than money. Ramón and Luisito petulantly announce that they are leaving, as neither girl pays them any attention. Adela firmly believes that Facundo is the right choice. Ramón wants to challenge Facundo, and Adela plans to get Facundo out of the house that night to avoid trouble. Attempting secretly to caution him in his room, she witnesses how Pepa and Facundo meet and discuss the carriage's being ready, but where is Rosita? While awaiting her, Facundo goes for the luggage, and Adela, from the darkness, wishes him a safe journey. Their exchange is interrupted by Mamerto, the Mayor. Facundo attempts to escape and Adela hides him. Confusion ensues and Don Rufo, in night clothes, finding Adela in Facundo's room, denounces the scandal. Rosa announces her plans to marry Facundo; even when he confesses he is Andrade, Rosa insists that she is his intended wife. Ramón wishes to punish Pepa and shoot Facundo, but Mamerto alleges the law protects the fugitive, and detains him. In the concluding scene, Rufo retrieves his money, then Ramón wins Adela.

This play seems to be an alternate version of *El caballero de industria*, previously discussed. This time Adela and her cousin Ramón are matched, without her resorting to a false claim of seduction. Rosa, not up in the clouds as was her counterpart Filomena of the other play, is modest, and thinking of becoming a nun. Facundo seems to be a real-life character; as Ramón says at the end, there are many such in Madrid. The critic López Funes finds the Facundo of *Los millonarios* superior to his counterpart in *El caballero de industria*.

La bondad sin la experiencia (Goodness without Experience), a three-act verse comedy performed at the Príncipe Theater on March 24, 1855, and published by Rodríguez the same year, is dedicated by the author to Pedro Calvo Asensio. The play takes place in Madrid, in the eighteenth century. On the second anniversary of the death of Guadalupe's husband, two suitors visit her (she and her sister Cecilia are Mexican). Diego seeks to tarnish the lady's reputation via his words to Fernando, a trusting soul who, intent on keeping things straight, manages to say the wrong thing most of the time. A series of cunning intrigues on the part of Diego, Guadalupe, and even Cecilia unexpectedly enable Fernando to win Guadalupe's hand. Fernando, depicted as none too bright, is used by others to achieve their own goals. He is not well defined, contrasting rather sharply with the vivacious and enterprising Diego and Guadalupe, so it is surprising that a woman should be so callous as to feed on the simplicity of Fernando, and ridicule him somewhat, if what she wanted was to marry him. I found no critique of this play.

Also in the decade of the 1850s García Gutiérrez wrote the librettos for several *zarzuelas*, which are commented upon in a subsequent chapter: *El grumete* (The Ship-boy), 1853; *La espada de Bernardo* (Bernard's Sword), 1853; *La cacería real* (Royal Hunt), 1854; *Azon Visconti*, 1858; *El robo de las sabinas* (The Rape of the Sabines), 1859; and *Cegar para ver* (To Become Blind in Order to See), 1859.

II Plays in the Decade 1860–1870

Eclipse parcial (Partial Eclipse), a verse comedy in three acts, was performed for the first time in the Príncipe Theater on December 24, 1863, and published the same year by Rodríguez. In Madrid, Count Martín visits his wife, Adela, who lives in the other half of their house, pending the outcome of their petition for annulment of their marriage. Francisco, a new servant, is admitted under the name of Tomás; he knew the maid, Isabel, years before. Adela tells her sister Sofía that she and Carlos should marry as soon as possible, but Sofía declines until her life is more settled. Carlos, arriving with the good news that he is now a full-fledged judge, agrees to help Sofía patch up her sister's marriage. Facundo Malespina (Bad-Omen), a gossipy friend of the Count, visits him after spending two years in Valencia. Antón Barragán, a cousin, also arrives: a young, conceited man, proud of his post with the government which he owes to the influence of his uncle, he irritates Malespina. Hearing of the impending separation, he thinks he may have a chance with Adela. With the arrival of the expected letter proclaiming the couple's freedom from each other, all go to celebrate their separate ways, but leave together. The servants Isabel and Francisco, wearing their masters' finery, also exit.

The following act, in a room adjoining the ballroom, finds Malespina and irritable Antón making small talk; they are joined by Adela and Sofía. After they stroll back to the dance floor, an angry Count Martín arrives. Having visited Carlota, for whom he left Adela, he found her with Carlos, in bedclothes. Martín shames Carlos, who tells Sofía in an aside that his plan is working; however, she looks annoyed. Facundo implies that the Count is upset about his advances to Adela, which leads to a challenge to a duel. Carlos will be witness.

In act three, Adela instructs the servants to say that she and her sister are not home if Carlos comes. The latter tells Count Martín he cares nothing for Carlota; he only wanted to teach Martín a lesson. The count is glad, but Carlos has lost Sofía's love. His lady appears, to say Adela should not have spoken for her, but she wants no clarification. Carlos explains he loved Carlota until he met Sofía; the other woman kept after him until she met Martín, and Carlos, free of her, wrote her with his plan to make the Count jealous, to which Carlota agreed. Count Martín ran where he was attracted, to his wife, whom he suddenly saw as a woman, and Facundo as a rival. Sofía, relieved, asks Carlos not to resort to such tactics in the future. Martín is happy to see Carlos and Sofía together again; she calls Adela and retires to a prudent distance to listen. Martín ponders how the separation and sudden reconciliation will look, but when Adela appears, extremely well dressed, he sees her as a woman once more. They pretend indifference, and Sofía makes impertinent remarks, finally telling them to stop pretending and join hands, which they do, allegedly in memory of the child they had, who died. Carlos comes in to ask them to embrace, and Sofía exhorts her brother-in-law not to defy God's law.

The predictability of this play, when Sofía asks Carlos to help her work to rejoin Adela and Martín is elusive because we find Sofía did not know of Carlos's plan, kept secret to be better carried out. Facundo, opportune in his arrival, is used, exploiting the bad concept everyone has of him. Characters derive lessons and examples from each other in this play, and Lomba y Pedraja terms *Eclipse parcial* moralizing.

III Venganza catalana *(Catalan Revenge)*

Venganza catalana, a four-act drama, in verse, first performed at the Príncipe Theater on February 4, 1864, honoring actress Matilde Díez, was published later the same year by Rodríguez. The first three acts take place in Andrinópolis, the last in Apros, in 1304. At night, as the work opens in the camp of the Alans, Irene goes to the tent of Gircón, under whose care she lives since her father's death, having been promised in childhood to Alejo, Gircón's son. She brings news of a Catalan prisoner who proves to be Alejo himself, long absent in search of the seducer of his sister Margarita. He is not a traitor, but found it necessary to join the Catalans in order to leave Sicily, and will serve his time as promised. His father frees him, but refuses to recognize him as a son until he returns as a

Greek. Alejo reminisces about his beloved María, married to another, and her voice is heard calling for help. When he goes to her aid, she recognizes his uniform as that of a soldier of Roger de Flor. Alejo refuses money as a reward, but asks for her handkerchief to cover his wound.

In the camp of the Masagets, Emperor Miguel Paleólogo, Gircón, and others discuss the advancing forces of Roger, victorious over so many Asians, barbarians, and Turks, feats for which Paleólogo envies him. Berenguer and Roger arrive with Catalan and Aragonese courtiers, ready to fight the infidel. Roger is revealed to be married to María, cousin of the Emperor. Alejo, who has kept his true identity from the Catalans, asks to be sent away. María appears, warning Roger about the Alans, who are not trustworthy: she suffered an attemped murder the night before. Roger promises to find her rescuer and reward him. He fears for her safety, but María refuses to leave the camp. Berenguer agrees to lodge the gentlemen and María in the city. Alejo and Irene talk about his young love, María, whom Irene believes is in the city; he faints from his wound and Irene sees the handkerchief.

Act two, in the palace at Andrinópolis, shows Berenguer telling of the triumphs of Roger, who is present, and how they should put down Emperor Paleólogo, jealous and envious. Perich de Naclara brings a soldier's complaint: they are not only not allowed in the city, but are paid in devaluated money. Naclara is therefore eager to leave the Emperor, but Roger tries to solve the problem peacefully. Paleólogo, confronted with his unfulfilled promises, makes clear he resents being embarrassed and having allied himself with the Alans. The others do not trust him; Berenguer considers the Catalan and Aragonese to be liberators, and the spoils belong to them. Roger disagrees: they went to the aid of those in trouble, not to conquer. Alejo and María meet by chance; their childhood love, she says, is a thing of the past; she is a Bulgarian princess, a detail he did not know before, and married to Roger de Flor. She disapproves of Miguel Paleólogo and the way he treats his people, and considers herself not Greek, but Spanish. Irene, who finds them talking, scolds her for not being one of them. Gircón appears after María has left, and Alejo is told that the man who dishonored Margarita is there; he is expected to kill him, but is not told his name. Later, the Emperor tells Gircón he has been inciting the Catalans so they will turn against Roger, who will be killed during a banquet.

Gircón offers to provide a young arm to accomplish the deed. Irene tries to implicate María and Alejo, but Roger pays no mind. Alone with María and Alejo, Roger relates the story of his first love, Margarita, whom he married secretly. He went to war and she believed herself abandoned. One day she saw the hermit who had blessed their union being led to the gallows: he was a criminal sheltered under the guise of a holy man. When she returned to her father, he repudiated her, and Margarita threw herself into the waters of the Bosporus. Roger came back from war to this tragic situation. As Alejo reveals that Margarita was his sister and the men embrace, Gircón informs Alejo it is almost time to avenge his sister and his honor. The young man says God will not ask him what he asked Cain; as for the one who "killed" Margarita (the father who provoked her suicide) Alejo has no strength against him.

Miguel in the third act tries to win over María and turn things against Gircón. Alejo brings news that Roger is safe and that the uprising is subsiding. Before his exit, Irene warns Alejo of Miguel's treason and confesses that she loves Roger, for which reason she wonders about Alejo and María's rekindling their love. When Roger enters, Irene reveals the early attachment of his wife and Alejo. The latter brings a parchment he stole from a messenger which asks for reinforcements to kill Roger and his allies. Roger doubts Alejo's sincerity when the latter advises him to flee, and he tests María to see what she thinks of Miguel. First suspecting that she is not loyal, he believes her when she swears her innocence in the name of the child she is going to have. Roger leaves for the banquet, where the treacherous act is carried out. Alejo regrets he cannot avenge Roger de Flor because that would mean killing his father. María, enraged with grief, exhorts the Catalans and Aragonese to take revenge, and she herself goes against Gircón.

In act four we learn how María, in mourning, is present at every scuffle and incites, with her presence, the drive of the Catalans to avenge Roger. Naclara explains to María Berenguer's plot to surprise the killer of her husband, but Berenguer is made prisoner. He gives an account of his mission and Paleólogo, astounded at his valor, wants to spare his life, which the prisoner refuses. María shames Miguel as a coward; if he wants to bring a guilty man to justice there is Gircón, an assassin. The latter reminds Miguel of his faithful service and asks to see Berenguer, free, out of the city. He requests that his son be left on watch inside the walls so he cannot interfere.

The Aragonese are so few that they can be counted as they kneel and pray in their camp under the banner of St. Peter. Miguel orders Alejo to stand watch, to his regret. María's presence startles Irene, who confesses her love for Roger. The dim light of dawn shows soldiers retreating, and the defeated troops bring the body of Gircón, at which María rejoices; Roger is avenged. Miguel Paleólogo, wounded, appeals to her, and she advises him, after he admits he is despicable, to flee. Aragonese and Sicilians scale the wall with pennants and the banner of St. Peter, as María praises those who carried out the Catalan revenge.

In the fourth edition of 1864 appear endnotes evidently included in the first edition, as well as the censor's authorization, signed by Antonio Ferrer del Río in November 1863. The nine notes refer to specific passages, sometimes quoted verbatim from historic accounts, notably those of Moncada and Muntaner, the former quoted in Castilian, the latter in Catalan. In the same edition there is a list of the cast who performed the play with the notation that it was done in honor of Matilde Díez. This seems likewise to be the occasion when friends and admirers of García Gutiérrez decided to dedicate to him a volume containing a selection of his plays. It also bears the inscription that the play is the property of the author, a sign that such rights were being enforced.

Fr. Blanco García finds the María of *Venganza catalana* very good, while Roger seems to him somewhat falsified. Nicholson Adams mentions Enrique Piñero, as did Lomba y Pedraja in 1925 and in his 1958 edition of the play, taking issue with García Gutiérrez for calling the Aragonese and Catalan soldiers of Roger de Flor "Spanish." Actually this is done only a few times during the play, and most of the time they are identified by their regional origins. What Piñero considers a rousing call for patriotism in the words of María at the end of the third act, as well as in some instances in the fourth, can also be construed as a shout for revenge or justice for the barbaric behavior of the cowardly Greek.

The outstanding character of the play is María, who, like most women created by García Gutiérrez, expresses herself in a proper, succinct, and lyric style which greatly enhances the image she evokes whereby a woman is a reflection of the man she loves. Later, hurt and enraged by the treachery of her people and the murder of her heroic husband, her language becomes direct, expressive, and strong, but never coarse, changing the mood and emotional state but not the person. Miguel Paleólogo, the Emperor, emerges as cowardly and envious, resentful of the man who rid his territory of the terrible Turks, capable of plotting the murder of his liberator and yet appealing to the patriotism of his cousin, widowed because of his treachery.

Of the youthful love of Alejo and María, little remains when he pledges allegiance to Roger (who had not seduced his sister without her consent, and subsequently had married her), knowing that María loves Roger and he deserves this love. His dilemma is whether to obey his father (indirectly responsible for Margarita's suicide) and thus kill Roger, who is not guilty. Torn between the duty to avenge his sister's apparent dishonor and death, and the need to point to the person responsible for the ultimate tragedy, his own father, Alejo remains loyal to both, and therefore distant from María. This decision leaves Alejo somewhat immersed in his personal sense of honor and family ties which pull him in different directions; therefore, he is an accessory to develop both parts of the plot, who does not shine in either, due to circumstances. It is this character in particular that García Gutiérrez must have invented for his love tangles in order to give the audience a dimension of emotion which would add to the historic account, which is the true attraction of the play.

What the historic consensus yields is that Roger de Flor was a Catalan, born in Tarragona in 1262. Lord and master of the Sicilian seas, the terror of Turks and Greeks, his help was very much in demand by kings and emperors. A crusader in Palestine, as Vice Admiral with 2,000 men he defended Andrónico Paleólogo from the Turks. In gratitude Andrónico offered Roger his niece as a wife, as well as riches. However, he soon became jealous of the man who had brought freedom and peace to his territories, since the weak Greeks were under the domination of their defenders, and in a conspiracy had Roger assassinated. Paleólogo also threatened his niece Karina, wife of Roger de Flor, with murder if she complained. The widowed woman instigated the indignant Catalan and Aragonese soldiers of Roger to avenge his death against the cowardly and ungrateful subjects of Paleólogo, who repaid his crusader liberator with treason.

According to the Enciclopedia Espasa-Calpe (volume 24, pp. 106–107) Roger de Flor was an Italian warrior born in Brindisi, Italy, in 1280, murdered in Andrinópolis in 1307, son of Ricardo de Flor, of German origin, a falconier of King Frederick II. Roger de Flor, a Knight Templar, later entered the service of Fadrique de Aragón,

King of Sicily. This information is more or less quoted by Nicholson Adams. However, if this be true, it is puzzling that the *Catalan Revenge* be so named, and that there are Catalan epics on the subject such as *Rondor de Llobregat,* by Rubió, *L'Orientada,* by Ruiz, *Lo camí del sol* (The Sun's Path), by Angel Guimerá, and a painting of Roger de Flor in Constantinople by José Moreno Carbonero, as well as several historic accounts aside from the chronicles of Moncada and Muntaner including Rubió y Lluch's *El ducado catalán en Atenas* (The Catalan Duchy in Athens, Barcelona, 1888); Bofarull's *Historia critica, civil y eclesiástica de Cataluña* (Critical, Civil and Eclesiastic History of Cataluña, Barcelona, 1878); Aulestia's *Historia de Catalunya* (Catalan History, Barcelona, 1887 and 1922). The extant account of how Roger came to be in the service of the king, and a crusader does not justify this identification with Catalans, unless he was really born in Tarragona as stated in the *Biografía Universal, Galería de Hombres Célebres* (Universal Biography, Famous Men), compiled by various authors and published by Bastiños, Barcelona, in 1880. Furthermore, if, as stated in the Espasa-Calpe, he was born in 1280, it is difficult to believe he commanded ships in 1291, at age eleven. Too many discrepancies exist between the two informative sources to believe Espasa.

The unfortunate accident of the fire in the house of his brother in Sevilla while García Gutiérrez was in London between 1855 and 1858 accounts for the fact that his original *Roger de Flor*, burned in that fire, later became *Venganza catalana.* What the author was able to reconstruct from memory and the influence of his greater experience undoubtedly combine in the resulting play. Lomba y Pedraja conceded, in his edition of this play, that it is impossible to give an accurate measure of the dramatic production of Antonio García Gutiérrez, but this play is one of his best. It received considerable public acclaim, epitomizing the maturity, mastery, artistry, and ever-present lyricism of its author. According to Palau y Dulcet, Federico Soler wrote a parody of this play, *La venganza de la Tana* (Tana's Revenge). Father Burguera lists such a title, termed "dangerous," in the second section of his book, giving the author as S. Pitarra, but without further details.

IV   Las cañas se vuelven lanzas (*The Reeds Turn into Spears*)

Las cañas se vuelven lanzas is a verse comedy in three acts, published by Rodríguez in 1864 and performed at the Príncipe

Theater. No performance date is given, but the work was approved December 17, 1863, for the censors by Antonio Ferrer del Río. The play takes place in Toledo, in the nineteenth century. In a room with a fireplace and arms on the walls Pedro, the innkeeper, oversees servants exchanging old furniture for new. Ana is a new guest, and since León has not paid in six months, he is being moved to the attic. Glad to hear his name, but pretending mere generosity, the lady has Blas, her butler, pay León's bill and make sure he receives plenty of money, as if it came from the innkeeper. Later Ana explains to Blas, and her maid, Clara, that León is her cousin with whom she grew up in the Canary Islands. She loves him and has been looking for him, but to test him she will pretend that her name is Cecilia and that Blas is her father.

León is puzzled by Pedro's treatment when the innkeeper gives him back his old, improved room. Fernando, another captain, brings him news of the new guest. Gaspar, León's aide, questioned by Clara, becomes suspicious; his master, alerted, decides to spy on the women. They are caught searching his room, for which Clara is blamed but pardoned. León tells Ana who he is, explaining that his uncle disowned his father, who died en route to Spain from the Canary Islands. He left behind a young cousin whom he loved, but she is now his enemy. Blas enters in the role of Cecilia's father, and in a comic scene takes her away, scolding her. Fernando and León celebrate the imminent conquest.

In the second act in Ana's house Blas complains, as he dusts, that the deceit should end, but Ana devises a complicated plot to conquer León and pry a firm commitment from him before revealing her real name. Blas takes full advantage of his newly acquired identity, doing as he pleases within the role. He speaks to Ana with the authority of a strict father, interferes with her interviews with León, and treats him as his equal while each is pretending to be what he is not: Blas a nobleman, León a tailor. The asides to and from Ana, meant to keep things in check, constitute a difficult scene, easily ruined by bad timing. The coarse speech of Blas seeps through no matter how elegant his clothes are. The farce requires Blas to discover León's plan to elope with Cecilia/Ana, and threaten that either León will marry his "daughter" or that they will kill each other. León accedes, asking Fernando to be his witness. The notary arrives, but after Ana signs she asks León to read the document before he signs. Upon seeing her real name León refuses to sign, alleging that her father caused the death of his own, so León will not inherit that money. Ana observes that their rancor leads nowhere, but he is inflexible. Fernando disagrees with his friend, and they argue.

The third act takes place in another part of Ana's house. León has been ill for days, and she has entered his room only when he is asleep; honor is his illness. Ana, who plans to go back to the Canary Islands, wants to take León with her, but does not know how. León appears in a daze, inquiring what has happened, just as Fernando is announced. Having previously wounded León in a duel, the latter was brought to Ana's house. The friends embrace and the visitor reminds León that he threw himself against his sword. León admits he did just that; he loves Ana, and wants to leave. Once more in Pedro's inn Blas, again in his true role, comes to tell León that Ana is despondent. He brings her papers for safekeeping, including one addressed to León from his uncle, a confession of his wrongdoing, wherein he admits being aware that Ana will pay the consequences, so she should not know. Touched, León later speaks to a seemingly absent Ana, who insists she remembers only the nice things. León burns the confession and they resolve to depart for Palma the next day, planning their wedding. Although there seems to be no critical material on this play full of intrigue, deceit, and display of feminine wiles, it too was included in the volume honoring García Gutiérrez.

V Juan Lorenzo

Juan Lorenzo, a verse drama in four acts published by Rodríguez in 1865, was performed for the first time December 18 of that same year at the Príncipe Theater. Occurring in Valencia in 1519, the play opens as Juan Lorenzo reads by a lamp in his house, although it is already daylight. The tools of his trade of wool dresser, a sword, and some religious items identify both his occupation and other inclinations. Bernarda scolds him for having spent the night without sleep, sick as he is; why study so much if he is only an artisan? Juan recalls Cardinal Cisneros and how much he learned from him, and the latter's opinion that Juan would make a mediocre monk but a superb soldier. In asides we learn Bernarda loves Juan Lorenzo; he later recalls with Guillén Sorolla that Bernarda was at his mother's side when she died. They have since lived as brother and sister. The girl goes to church and Sorolla informs Juan that he is in danger; a gentleman plans to kill him because they both love the same woman; further proof of how the nobility abuses the working class since Cardinal Cisneros died. Juan wants to stand up for their rights.

The Marchioness of Biar, whom Lorenzo's mother once breast-fed, comes to complain that Bernarda flirts with her brother, who in turn courts her, thereby causing family problems, as he has broken his engagement to a noblewoman. Vicente, a packsaddle maker, rushes in telling of trouble: at the church door, the Marchioness's brother tried to abduct a young woman and was struck from his horse. Juan Lorenzo leaves and later returns with Bernarda. The other men discuss their guilds' organizing against the nobility, while Bernarda appeals for peace. When the Count arrives, Juan stops him with his sword. The Count protests that he only wants to ask Bernarda for her forgiveness; she rejects him, as well as Guillén Sorolla's love.

In the courthouse in act two, groups of people await the ruling against the Count. The leader of the guilds want Juan Lorenzo to be their leader, and amid such talk he and Bernarda arrive, followed shortly by the Marchioness and her servant Francin. The Count appears to hear his sentence, an unwise move, given the mood of the mob. Francin enters with the verdict: the nobleman is sentenced to pay the girl 500 ducats. Lorenzo complains of the freedom given the Count in a long speech; the oppressive nobility must be fought with force. He calls for them to form a *germanía* (brotherhood) of thirteen leaders, in memory of Our Lord Jesus Christ and his twelve apostles. The Marchioness asks Bernarda to appease the people, but she fears that Juan Lorenzo will think ill of her. The noble lady tries the same thing with Juan, hinting that Bernarda loves him. Juan tests Bernarda with the suggestion that he may return to the monastery, which she does not believe. What if they were to marry? Finally they declare their love for each other, but the wedding will have to be postponed because Sorolla announces the group will sail at once for Barcelona to see the king. The guilds are ready to rebel, wishing to try the Count again. The latter enters with his sister and Francin, and Bernarda forgives the Count; Juan Lorenzo approves, but Sorolla maintains that the insult affects all of them. Lorenzo prevails in that the Count will be judged again, but meanwhile he is let free into the custody of his sister. Sorolla states he will not stand by Juan Lorenzo if they are drawn to opposite sides.

Act three opens in the house of Juan Lorenzo, now suspect in the eyes of Vicente and Sorolla, who have seen Francin enter the house. The king agreed to respect the Valencian *fueros* (rights), but the nobility prevailed upon the king, who went back in his word. Lorenzo wants to kill the power but without bloodshed. He realizes ignorance is equally evil, but his friends do not. Upset, sickly, exhausted by the journey, he falls on a chair, sensing he will die soon. He had a dream in which, trying to save a sheep from a lion, he awoke a hyena, which killed the shepherd; he ran, and a mob gathered to see him pass, with a head on a spear. Bernarda concludes that the dream is a warning from God. After Juan Lorenzo leaves, the Count arrives to see him, but finds Bernarda instead. She pleads with him to flee, insisting that she does not love him. Some townspeople inform them that the sentence is death if the Count does not marry the girl. Bernarda says she has rejected his marriage proposal and requests to see the judges. Sorolla is amazed and indignant; Juan Lorenzo has indeed awakened the hyena.

As act four begins, Juan Lorenzo laments that his rectitude has cost him Bernarda and their happiness. Sorolla tells him there is hope; she is not yet married, so he will stop the Count and wipe out the nobility; not in vain is he the leader of the mob, which will obey him. Vicente brings news of an attack on Juan Caro, one of the "thirteen"; there must be traitors around. Behind Juan Lorenzo's back, Vicente and Guillén Sorolla plot to make believe he was assassinated by a nobleman, thereby enraging the mob. Bernarda walks into the room as they leave and the Marchioness of Biar appears, seeking shelter; because of her brother the palace was attacked. Lorenzo, sad and ill, plans to leave so as not to see the wedding, but Bernarda protests. Upon the Count's arrival, Juan advises him to leave the city if he wants peace. Francin brings the rumor of Sorolla's death, for which the Count, the viceroy, and other noblemen are accused. Trading capes with Francin, the Count agrees to leave, and Juan Lorenzo guides them out of the city.

Vicente, after receiving news of an inheritance, is no longer considered one of the people. The mob is enraged by the false rumor, which Vicente will try to rectify. A horrified Juan Lorenzo returns, relating that Francin was killed by the mob while wearing his master's cape; the priest of St. Nicholas, who tried to aid him, was also killed. Francin's head was speared; all this is Sorolla's doing. Lorenzo is so repulsed and indignant he cannot think of his own wedding; he hurts too much, emotionally and physically. The Marchioness tries to persuade him not to disappoint Bernarda again, but he is more concerned with the people and those who are so unruly. As the noble lady goes to see Bernarda, Juan Lorenzo reflects on his shattered dreams of freedom and respect for the people, his limitations for accomplishing such an enterprise, and his failing health. Sensing the approach of death, and unable to rally, he expires.

When the women return they first think he is asleep, but soon discover he is dead. As Bernarda refuses to believe it, the Marchioness separates her from him, and draws the curtains, sheltering from view the armchair where he lies. Guillén Sorolla brings tidings that the mob has turned against Juan Lorenzo because he is friendly with the nobility. The women tell him Juan is asleep, then let Guillén see what he has done: wounded him in his soul. The Marchioness urges Sorolla to vindicate himself by controlling the mob, nearing the house, and the women pray as Guillén Sorolla goes to face the people.

The ending suggests that some reaction will take place, perhaps for the good, when the crowd sees Sorolla alive, but his unthinking, drastic ways of inciting the ignorant will leave their mark on him. Part of his behavior is triggered by his frustrated love for Bernarda. She in turn has a difficult time warding off the Count, combating Sorolla's jealous tongue, and expressing her love for Juan Lorenzo without seeming forward, in the hope he will reciprocate. Juan Lorenzo abandoned his religious training to defend the trampled artisan class from the abuses of a semiforeign king, whose jurisdiction over certain Spanish territories was neither well defined nor properly administered. His ideals are quite removed from the love he feels for Bernarda, with whom he has lived as a brother, so that another kind of affection is out of the question. The Marchioness of Biar is a tempering force, intervening with propriety and discretion; she is a link between her plebeian friends, almost related to Juan Lorenzo, and the abusive nobility represented by her brother the Count.

García Gutiérrez has woven in a love element to bring to life on the stage a page from the history of Spain and the kingdom of Valencia. There are perhaps unjustified exits from the stage, on the part of Juan Lorenzo especially, the motivation being occasionally unclear; someone else reports subsequently on the events which called him away. Various people later converge in Lorenzo's house to inform the others. The three men extracted from the "thirteen" reflect three stages of the guild's uprising: Vicente, who has rich relatives, is not destitute, and is therefore more inclined to be swayed by Juan Lorenzo's ideals but also by the down-to-earth thinking of the impetuous Sorolla, who believes in taking justice by force, not selectively or judiciously. All those elements, latent in the historical times of the *germanías,* 1519 to 1522, actually did cause the death of the real-life Juan Lloréns, already in poor health. Those who find his death inglorious in the play fail to see that in this case García Gutiérrez did not juggle historic accounts. Juan Lloréns was a real-life hero, the truth of whose achievements and ideals was emphasized and interrupted by his death. There was no reason to dramatize it further by inventing a fictional violent episode.

The case of *Juan Lorenzo* differs from that of the other plays in that, according to more than one critic (some perhaps quoting an earlier opinion or influenced by other's observations), it was not successful on stage, yet is possibly the author's best. So state Lomba y Pedraja, Juan Alcina, and Lewis E. Brett. Coming soon after *Venganza catalana,* they say, another patriotic play was expected, but instead of a rousing cry for freedom, *Juan Lorenzo* proved to be a warning of what an unchecked revolutionary movement could cause: indiscriminate bloodshed, with the innocent punished along with the guilty. Nicholson Adams regrets that García Gutiérrez did not continue in the vein of what he terms "serious character drama." Lomba and Brett consider *Juan Lorenzo* a finished psychological study, better appreciated when read than if seen in the theater (albeit that is the purpose for which it was created in the first place). The character of Bernarda is discussed by Lomba at some length; he is amazed at the dignity, good judgment, and other virtues attributed to a girl with no evident formal education or culture, yet full of dignity, moral qualities and modesty. This type of woman is not so rare, but García Gutiérrez seems to have distributed all those assets between a noblewoman, as he depicts the Marchioness of Biar, and a woman who is almost a maid. Alcina is of the opinion that Bernarda represents Spain, given to despotic noblemen at the beginning of the drama and regenerated at the end. Father Burguera in his book reiterates Father Blanco García's evaluation of *Juan Lorenzo* as being a beautiful and eloquent drama.

Reputed to be the play that most satisfied its author, *Juan Lorenzo* met with difficulties from the beginning, as the censor did not permit its performance on the grounds that it had political overtones, and because it was a good drama. García Gutiérrez's vigorous protest brought rectification of this ruling, but the advance notice of such opposition of necessity worked against the play. In the 1865 edition of *Juan Lorenzo*, printed by Rodríguez, there is a note preceding the text of the censor's forbidding its performance,[2] followed by a governmental order to form a committee to examine the play in view of the protest lodged by García Gutiérrez. Another document reproduced reports the favorable result of such action.

Narciso Serra, the censor in question, born in 1830, is described as short, blond, blue-eyed, pleasant, hard-of-hearing, and a mediocre actor. He wrote poems and comedies, publishing a volume of poetry at age sixteen. Given to gambling, women, and dedicated to the pursuit of revelry and carousing, he left the army and worked in the Ministry of Government. His dissipated life caused an attack of paralysis. In 1864, confined to his home, he was given the post of theatrical censor, until the revolutionary government ended that. Undoubtedly suffering mental lapses and other disorders due to his paralytic condition, he prohibited *Juan Lorenzo* because of its political slant, adding the observation that it was a good drama. García Gutiérrez took his protest to the highest places and obtained permission to present his play, but under the shadow of the preliminary troubles. The early critics, therefore, describe the play as not very good theater, while failing to criticize the author on other grounds than that he really respected the historic figure of the protagonist.

Historically, the times of the *germanía* wars were too complicated to allow sweeping statements applicable to all of Spain, thereby blaming the uprising solely on the misgovernment of Charles V, I of Spain. In Castile the target was the king himself, while in Valencia it was oppression by the nobility. In the archives of the University of Valencia, among many manuscripts and documents, there is a reference to three unusual happenings in that city in 1517, taken as prophecies of ills that occurred later: a great fire appeared in the sky and posed itself at the top of the Miguelete tower; the Turia River overflooded; and a lion roamed the streets for several days. Two years later came the communal war, and the Moors of Gandía, Oliva, and Llombay asked to be baptized, out of fear; then they had to observe their new religion or face expulsion. Locust plagues and pestilence occurred during the year whose date marks the beginning of the *germanía* wars (1519) after Charles I became heir to the Spanish throne. Queen Germana, widow of King Fernando el

Católico, was then Vicereine of Valencia. After many festivities there came pestilence and earthquakes, taken by the population as signifying punishment from God, visited upon the nobility and aristocracy because of their exploitation of the poor. Many wealthy people fled, and the guilds started their revolt, instigated by Juan Lloréns, whose only aim was to achieve respect for the rights of the working class. In memory of Christ and the twelve apostles, he headed a group of thirteen leaders from different guilds and occupations with the idea of defending the artisan, putting an end to dishonesty, and baptizing the Moors.

After a commission went to Barcelona to transmit the idea to the king, he approved, cautioning them to make good use of their weapons. Other delegates warned the king of the danger of arming the plebeians, so the sovereign retracted his word and forbade assemblies without the presence of the governor. This time Juan Lloréns himself and two of the "thirteen" visited the king promising allegiance to him as a king in Valencia before he signed the *fueros* (rights), so Charles I restored to them the right to bear arms. Later he sent an emmissary to swear to respect the *fueros*, but the Valencians demanded that the king come in person and make the oath to respect them.

Impatient, the rebels in Sagunto killed a number of nobles. Queen Germana was absent at the time, so the king sent Cardinal Diego Hurtado de Mendoza as Viceroy. He and the "thirteen" disagreed, while the townspeople continued to exterminate noblemen indiscriminately. Juan Lloréns, his health failing and undermined by his troubles, died of a broken heart after having seen Francí's head speared. The guild movement degenerated into a civil war, and there was no peace until All Saints Day, November 1, 1521. A mysterious young man, who claimed to be the legitimate heir to the throne, came from Castille, helping to prolong the war. He was Enrique Manrique de Lara, known as the "rei encobert" (king in disguise), upon whose place in history García Gutiérrez wrote the play *El Encubierto de Valencia,* already discussed. It was not until 1526, with Queen Germana as Vicereine, and with her new husband, the Duke of Calabria, that Valencia knew good government again. Carlos I did not visit Valencia for the first time until 1527. It is somewhat puzzling that García Gutiérrez would treat the story of the "undercover king" first, and not write a play dealing with the earlier part of the conflict until twenty-five years later. It will be observed that García Gutiérrez favored historical plots dealing with the Mediterranean Sea as a whole, not necessarily one of its shores.

From the 1860s there are also several *zarzuelas,* to be discussed in the corresponding chapter: *Llamada y tropa* (Call and Troop), 1861; *Galán de noche* (Night Suitor), 1862; *La tabernera de Londres* (The Tavern Keeper Girl of London), 1862; *La vuelta del corsario* (The Return of the Pirate), 1863, and *El capitán negrero* (The Slave-Dealer Captain), 1865.

CHAPTER 6

The Last Plays

I Sendas opuestas (*Opposite Paths*)

SENDAS opuestas is a verse comedy in three acts, published by Rodríguez in 1871 and performed the same year on March 22 at the Español Theater, honoring actress Salvadora Cayron. Acts one and three occur in a small Scottish town; the second act is set in London, during times contemporary to the author. In his house, Morton, a well-to-do farmer, plays cards with others while his daughter Berta, raised in Louisiana, talks to Jorge, rejecting his love, because she is engaged to Tomás. It is her birthday, and as Berta's cousin Luisa is heard murdering a piece at the piano, the card game ends. Guillermo complains to Jorge about how badly Luisa plays, and a bet ensues: he undertakes to lure her from her mother's house. Jorge counts on a mulatto, Salomé, to help his cause. Tomás gathers enough courage to tell Berta, and then her father, that the engagement is off. Morton takes it very well. In an aside Tomás wishes that Luisa would pay attention to him. Morton and his sister Isabel (Luisa's mother) differ in the way they raise their children. Berta announces that Luisa has fainted (according to Guillermo's plan) and tells Jorge she is free. He must now talk to her father or he need not come back. Jorge dislikes the hint of a wedding, and Guillermo tells him Luisa resisted until he told her he was a count, so he advises telling Berta that Jorge is also a nobleman. Luisa is taken home and the party ends; Morton questions Berta about her break with Tomás and whether she has not given cause. After all retire, Salomé admits Jorge, to Berta's anger. Morton ejects Jorge, meeting Isabel on her way in. Luisa had told her mother that both cousins were planning to leave home; Morton scolds Berta, who claims innocence, but her father orders her to

112

The Last Plays

leave his house rather than dishonor him. Isabel informs her brother that she met Luisa on her way out, but the girl repented and chose to stay with her mother rather than go with a gentleman that awaited her. Deciding to speak to Berta, they find her room empty and the balcony open. Isabel is grateful she saved her daughter.

In act two, in London, Toby, a servant, tells Salomé two gentlemen wish to see the lady of the house. Jorge arrives and we learn through him that Berta goes out of the house every day, but he does not know where. Jorge's father suspects that he loves her. Berta fears Salomé, who knows her secret. She is in a peculiar situation: Jorge's father is coming to meet her, and she in turn wrote her father saying they are married. Jorge is displeased, but instructs Salomé to remain silent about Berta, supposedly a wealthy widow. The mulatto maid, alone, remembers Berta slapped her and plans to make her pay for it. Morton and Tomás, ridiculously overdressed, enter, awed by the luxury they see; Morton is startled to find Salomé, freed by him when she was a slave. Guillermo and Lord Seymour, Jorge's father, arrive to see Berta. Guillermo tells the older gentleman fantastic lies about Berta's origin. The visit is interrupted by the strangely dressed Morton and Tomás. Upon discovering Morton's identity, Lord Seymour says his son cannot marry a woman of such low birth; gathering she is not married, Morton disowns her. When all leave, Berta screams upon finding Salomé by her side saying that they are even.

The last act shows Morton's house with the room as it was before Berta left. Tomás, glad that he married Luisa, reads Morton a letter given him at the door: a woman dying in a hospital wants to see Morton. Certain it is his daughter, Morton leaves. Berta enters by another door and finds Tomás, who inquires sarcastically about her wealth and high living. She says that her father is her last refuge, and Morton returns from the hospital, having seen Salomé, who confessed how badly she treated Berta. Tomás, who had gone to recall Morton, reappears, having learned that Berta was not to blame for the attempted abduction of Luisa. Next, Lord Seymour arrives; Morton pretends not to know him. The gentleman offers Berta a dowry, and she is offended. He then offers marriage, but Morton, to his daughter's dismay, says they are not equal. Jorge enters; after much talk about who is better and nobler, with Morton set in his negative position, Jorge declares he has renounced his wealth in favor of his brother. Then all consent to the wedding, and the couple will live with Morton. Lomba y Pedraja finds this to be a play both of character and social thesis.

II Nobleza obliga (*Nobility Obliges*)

Nobleza obliga is a three-act comedy, published in 1872 by López Vizcaíno, performed at the Circo Theater on January 25, 1872. As a preface, the author states he had completed the idea for this play and started to write it when, due to political incidents in 1868, he had to travel outside the country, interrupting his writing, which he resumed in 1870, in Genoa. Once in Madrid he learned Antonio Hurtado had written a one-act play whose main theme was identical to a scene of the second act of *Nobleza obliga*. García Gutiérrez considered cutting the scene out, but finally decided to leave it in, since removing it would harm the continuity of the play. This could not hurt Hurtado's play, which had been already published, and if anyone accused García Gutiérrez of plagiarism it would not damage him much, being at the end of his career. This account is dated in Genoa, December 1871.

The first act begins in Doña Francisca's house; she is surprised to find strangers waiting for her upon her return. These are Doña María del Barco and her old servant, Gil. Doña Francisca is a young widow, and Doña María's son, Luis, loves her. She makes it very clear she does not care for Luis, since she loves another man. María is hurt to think someone might reject her son, but relieved at Francisca's frankness. When the visitors leave, Nicolasa, the maid, brings Sancho out of hiding, to Francisca's anger. He also comes on behalf of Don Luis; the day before her suitor Don Diego found him there and threw him down the stairs, an incident about to be repeated with the arrival of Diego and Gil. Diego inquires of Francisca, in very dry tones, about his rival and Sancho; he is not ready to marry yet. Francisca insists she loves him, but his jealousy is not good. When Sancho is discovered and again bounced down the stairs, Francisca tells Diego a drawn sword is improper in her house; he is not her husband and has no rights. She sends him out of her life.

Outside, Don Gregorio del Barco informs Diego that his royal grant (*encomienda*) has arrived. Diego rejoices; this will give him more leverage to defeat his rival and take revenge on Don Luis de Trejo. Gil observes that Francisca does not love Luis, so why not

The Last Plays 115

leave him alone? Gregorio tries also to calm him; Diego is like a son to him, and Luis is his nephew. However, when Diego returns to see Francisca, a note wrapped around a rock comes through the balcony, thrown by Don Luis; Diego wants to kill him. Francisca blocks the door, leaves, and locks it from the outside. Nicolasa, under threats, brings another key and frees Diego. Shortly afterwards a scream is heard and the maid extinguishes the light.

In the second act María, praying with her servants, wants to send Luis to Italy and separate him from the hopeless love that has him in such a sad state. Gil tells her that the rival is Diego Abarca, whose mother, Inés de Maldonado, died years before. As his father did not love the child, Diego and Luis were raised by the same wet nurse in Buitrago, but the children never got along. Sancho enters, taking a long time to say his master will be late, but when Doña María retires he tells Gil he left Luis in front of Doña Francisca's house. Hearing a scream he ran to see the cause, but it was another man. Don Gregorio arrives asking urgently to speak to his sister, confessing he loved Inés de Maldonado, but her parents opposed their plans and gave her in marriage to Pedro Abarca. María remembers; what nobody knew was that Inés was pregnant at the time. Pedro, jealous and suspicious, hated the child; the mother tried not to show love for him. Thus Diego and Luis met in infancy. With Doña Inés and Pedro dead, Gregorio does not want Diego to know of his illegitimacy. The trouble is, Diego and Luis love the same woman, as María knows. Francisca arrives, reporting Luis has challenged Diego to a duel; she locked the latter in her house and seeks Gregorio, who goes to see what he can do. María asks Francisca to write her a letter detailing why she rejects Luis, so he will see the proof and stop pursuing her. As Francisca goes to the next room to write, Diego enters, seeking shelter; having killed a man in a duel, he is pursued by the authorities. María agrees to hide him, but Francisca returns and informs Diego that María is Luis's mother. After María learns the truth, she wants to go to her son, but duty comes first. The authorities call on her, and she finds it very difficult not to give Diego to them. She wants him out of her house and punished, and after he and Francisca are in the street, María calls from the balcony that the fugitive is around, and the search party goes after him, to Gregorio's dismay.

In act three Gil finds it admirable that Gregorio wants to put in a good word for Diego, but Doña María has gone to the palace and will be heard. Gregorio cannot tell Gil that Diego is his son. All of Madrid is angry at the killing, and Diego is sentenced to die the next day. Gil is puzzled by all this goodness; Luis was Gregorio's nephew. María, returning from the palace, scolds her servant for letting anyone in, even her brother. She clamors for justice but then reasons that perhaps Luis had harmed somebody. Francisca finds her way in to plead with María; the latter reminds her she turned a deaf ear when María pleaded for her son. As Gregorio enters, Francisca points out that he forgives the killer and tries to intercede on Diego's behalf. María exhorts her brother to tell the truth, and not receive praise he does not deserve; he appeals to her nobility, and she observes that such titles have to be earned, not merely inherited. That is the duty that binds nobility. Gil forces a story on them: two children, almost identical, were brought to Buitrago and a nurse was bribed to switch them, so that after all Luis was not María's son. She reacts by being more hurt, since she lavished her love on a stranger. However, when the names are revealed she wants to see Diego, and maybe save him. Francisca is overjoyed, but not Gregorio. María composes a letter for the king which Gregorio goes to deliver. María cannot suddenly feel love for Diego, but must change her mourning clothes to see him; when he arrives, confused, Gregorio makes clear he will deal with him later, having learned he is the father of the dead youth.

María sees Diego alone. He knows everything and wants to kiss her hand, but she refuses; his is stained with blood. She felt nothing when she saw him after learning he was her son, yet her heart always told her when Luis was near. Diego's affection and veneration, in turn, are for the mother who showed him no love. They agree their feelings cannot change, and María reminds Diego that he has the love of a woman. He doubts Francisca, and María defends her. As Diego rejoices in his good fortune, Gregorio enters, calling him Luis and reminding him of the murder of his cousin; he laments having raised a viper. Diego replies it is his fault for giving him so much. Gregorio seeks a duel with him, but the young man refuses. Gil returns, confessing he cannot swear to what he said earlier; he made up the story in order to lessen María's pain and save Diego, who is elated; Gregorio is not. Diego wants to tell María, who is happy but offended, feeling a new pain. She cannot retract her word, as a member of the nobility, but she does not wish to see Diego or Francisca ever again. María dresses in mourning once more and the others leave her to mourn, remember, and weep; she now calls her sorrow happiness.

At the beginning, both women seem strong-willed and unafraid to speak. Doña María loves her son blindly, and cannot imagine anyone not liking him, yet the woman causing all his suffering is deaf to her plea. Francisca enjoys the freedom of being a widow, likes parties, and comes and goes as she pleases, without exposing herself to undue gossip. Luis, entangled in overpowering feelings, believes his persistence will prevail in the end, but his opponent is formidable. Diego, jealous and ill-tempered, is prone to draw conclusions purely from appearances or suspicion; his drastic actions against Sancho and Luis are conducive to no good, since Francisca loves him and does not merit the abuse, nor is she willing to take it. Gregorio, guarding his secret, tries to reason with Diego and help him, as does Francisca, but it is María, whose humanity, sensibility, and charity he receives even after she knows he is the killer of her son. The emotions she feels, the fair-minded thoughts she brings forth in an effort to temper her grief, balancing her sorrow, justice, and revenge, are a true challenge for any actress, especially considering the story Gil invents. Both women, with their strong characters, reach a level of understanding because of that very trait, but it is María who emerges as an indisputably great creation by García Gutiérrez. Diego has learned much and will, no doubt, reform, but there is some sense of injustice in his going free to marry Francisca, when his quick temper caused the death of Luis, which will go unpunished. Luis, persistent in his hopeless love, his only "crime," leaves María immersed in sadness and a vast emptiness.

III Doña Urraca de Castilla

Doña Urraca de Castilla, a verse comedy in three acts, was first performed on October 15, 1872, at the Circo Theater. The second edition, by López Vizcaíno, 1872, is bound together with a critical appraisal by "Marcelo," who dedicates it to an unidentified *Soledad* (this essay is dated 1872 as well, and published the same year by Berenguillo). After twenty-four performances, the critic wants to give his opinion so as not to influence those who applauded the play. The preliminary words promise a thrashing; Marcelo holds that critics should be lenient to a novice author, but once he reaches the end of the road to fame they should be just, even if *Doña Urraca* was being celebrated even before it was staged (which was done very well). Marcelo notes that when the drama was finished it had no title. The actress who performed one of the leading roles suggested "The Two Mothers," while the author preferred the name Urraca, a queen who would evoke historic pages; however, García Gutiérrez avoids the episode of her love for Don Gómez, already dead at the start of the play. She calls herself his mother, but the courtiers and even King Alfonso, her husband, know their relationship was impure.

Marcelo points out that García Gutiérrez dignified the queen but was less kind to King Alfonso, deforming what historic accounts say of both. Showing the king in a bad light is adjudged a "black cloud" that diminishes the brilliant verse, some beautiful passages, and well-defined characters. Marcelo resents King Alfonso's being shown as a common criminal to the detriment of the author of the play. Planning the murder of his infant stepson and having it carried out, is as bad as having vassals reproach his action since both of these actions debase the king. The critic dedicates several pages to showing that García Gutiérrez made motherly love the central theme of the play, but chose a bad vehicle in Urraca as a queen; improving her image somewhat, tarnished that of her husband even more. The historic part, then, is the erroneous element here; ordinary people would have been better suited for enacting the theme than the monarchs. Given the historic setting, the nurse who tries to save Prince Alfonso is deemed too learned and vocal for her station in life (such characters abound in the theater of García Gutiérrez), further debasing the nobility by placing it at a lower level of intelligence. In the fifty-five pages of the critique, a long list of faults is expressed in progressively harsher tones, with many repetitions. Marcelo concludes that it is only the poet who may be applauded in this play—that is, its lyric aspect alone, not the dramatic or historic.

Marcelo's critique was printed in the newspaper *El Tiempo* on November 13, 1872. Surprisingly, he did not undertake similar scrutiny of other plays by García Gutiérrez or of his contemporaries. Perhaps his task would have been too cumbersome. Perhaps the play's being by a mature dramatist and not a beginner prompted this critique, or possibly Marcelo was especially well versed in that particular segment of Spanish history. Be that as it may, the severe critic himself states the theme of the play, and as in so many of García Gutiérrez's works the historic background is just that, a canvas upon which variations of the real theme are woven, in this case the theme of motherly love. This sentiment causes the author to idealize a notoriously indiscreet queen because of her condition of a mother, relegating her husband to a secondary place, and tarnishing his accomplishments and character by making him her enemy.

Worth noting is the fact that Matilde Díez, a famous actress in her day, did not play Doña Urraca, but performed the role of Sancha, the nurse, one of the two "mothers" for whom the actress wanted to name the play. This subtheme underlines the author's intention to make maternal sentiment the main force of his play, as well as the contention of the critic that the historicity of the royal characters was considerably altered. Marcelo assesses rather accurately the theme, defects, and beauties of this play, based largely on the life of Alfonso (later King Alfonso VII), the son of Ramón de Borgoña and Urraca of Castilla, who was married for the second time to King Alfonso I of Aragon, called "The Warrior." Alfonso did not hesitate to act against his own wife (no model of good conduct) in order to further his possessions. The child, saved from a plot to kill him, later became king. In another critical opinion, Father Blanco García concurs that Alfonso is somewhat falsified in this play. Eugenio Maximino Hartzenbusch offers the information that "Marcelo" was the pen-name of José de Cárdenas, whose critiques and reviews appeared in the newspaper *El Tiempo*.

IV Crisálida y mariposa (*Chrysalis and Butterfly*)

Crisálida y mariposa, a light piece in two acts and in verse written for the actress Elisa Boldún, was performed on November 9, 1872, in the Español Theater, and published by López Vizcaíno the same year. In the garden of a house near Valencia, Clara dresses a doll which Ruperta is holding. Fifteen years old, Clara is too big to play with dolls, but very unruly and opinionated. She resents her aunt and uncle, with whom she lives, because they want her to wear a long dress instead of a short skirt and pants, and are seeking a husband for her. Clara leaves the doll to her cousin Marcial, in order to take her hated piano lesson, with every intention of ruining the keys. Fernando, the intended bridegroom, arrives, to Marcial's dismay; they were friends, but did not know about Clara. Fernando's heart is elsewhere, but his father wants the match. The boys agree to make Clara dislike Fernando, in favor of Marcial. Aunt Nemesia and Uncle Pablo, an entomologist, arrive and greet Fernando. Nemesia speaks in language similar to Archie Bunker's while Pablo compares Clara to a chrysalis in her present state; soon she will become a butterfly. Fernando likes the girl, but finds it silly for her to play the piano after dinner. Why, when there are guitars? He is from Sevilla. Aunt Nemesia asks Clara to play for Fernando, who chooses an "infernal gallop"; an exchange of harsh concepts follows; according to Clara only people, not animals, understand certain things. True, says Fernando, and they are cured by a good wallop, or so Clara deducts. She agrees to marry Fernando only if Marcial will live with them. He says her cousin is about to marry someone else, and she is jealous. In a soliloquy ending the first act, Clara realizes that she has discovered tears and jealousy, that people and animals go in pairs, and that she is in love.

In act two Nemesia knits in the garden as Fernando and Marcial talk, sitting on a bench. Clara is hostile to Marcial, but she may come around. Nemesia describes women as "perfection" while Pablo considers them "parasites." The lady decides to take Marcial shopping for Clara's trousseau, so Fernando and Clara may talk. When Clara appears, wearing a long dress but with the doll dangling at her side, Fernando (remembering his Andrea in Triana), flees into the house. Ruperta laboriously extracts from Clara that it is Marcial who is causing her unrest. Marcial evades Aunt Nemesia and the young cousins clarify their feelings. However, Fernando was the instigator of the lie about Marcial's supposed wedding, so Clara wants to test his scheme; Marcial leaves in anger, and Clara confronts Fernando. In a mixture of calculated innocence and flirtation she picks up her music and drops it one piece at a time as she walks, so he will have to pick up the sheets, thereby testing his opinion of love and women. Fernando comes to find her budding womanhood more appealing than Andrea's charms, and declares his love for Clara, who then mentions his love in Sevilla. She flirts with Fernando until Aunt Nemesia appears, and the girl leaves. Fernando tries to explain that Clara has matured and has come to realize she loves Marcial. Nemesia summons her husband when she sees Fernando will not stand in the way of Marcial, and Pablo agrees to the match. In that scene, woman is compared to a butterfly whose

The Last Plays

wings will do her no good in marriage if her husband clips her feet. Clara's last speech expresses doubt as to becoming a butterfly, wondering if she is doing the right thing.

The title is accurate, for the play is indeed about an adolescent emerging from a childhood to which she clings stubbornly. García Gutiérrez portrays the two young men in such a way that until the end it is not predictable what Clara will do. Her uncle, a bit in the clouds, uses the terminology of his own science to describe women, unintentionally painting a poetic picture. His wife, mispronouncing words in a most natural way, brings to mind similar types, not totally illiterate but unfamiliar with books. In the specific case of Nemesia, she could well be a Valencian, as depicted, used to hearing and saying words slightly different in her vernacular, and not totally at ease in Castilian. The author seems to have portrayed people he actually knew at some point in his life, not necessarily in the circumstances described, but who left enough of an impression on him to wish to put them on stage. Nicholson Adams is less appreciative, classifying this play as a "lifeless comedy."

V Un cuento de niños (*A Children's Tale*)

Un cuento de niños is a verse comedy in two acts, published by Rodríguez in 1877 and performed at the Español Theater on November 23 of the same year. The first act takes place in Burgos, the second in Pozuelo de Aravaca, about 1860. At an inn in Burgos Esteban tries to convince his daughter Cecilia that she should at least meet her intended father-in-law, without revealing who her father is, before rejecting the marriage arrangement. Among other things, Cecilia must have music ready, but not Verdi's; his music is for deaf people.[1] Esteban leaves on an important errand, and Miguel sneaks in to see Cecilia. Secretly married, they live in fear, separated and terrified that her father will find out: his father knows and disapproves. Antonio, a servant, cautions that Esteban is coming, and Miguel hides in room number 2, whose occupant is out. Suddenly returning, she stops to talk to those present. She is from Madrid, the governess of a bad-tempered widower who keeps the portrait of his beautiful wife covered; her master has been waiting, for the past thirty years, for the visit of a friend on his name day, St. Servando, and he is preparing for it again this year, on the morrow. Esteban, visibly disturbed by the news, takes Cecilia away.

Gregoria, the governess, continues talking until Servando calls her, evincing his bad disposition, with orders to pack. Her shouts reveal she has found someone hiding in her room. Miguel comes out and there is a confrontation with Servando, who proves to be his father, speaking in rather formal and icy tones. The marriage without consent is one issue between them. Miguel recalls he left home because of the mystery of the portrait, and asks what Servando is doing in Burgos, other than spying on him. Servando refuses to explain and leaves in a rage, running into Cecilia. Miguel reveals that Servando is his father, who will not forgive him; Esteban, who joins them, wants to know why Miguel follows them. Painfully they confess they are married, and Esteban reacts accordingly. Very angry at first, he is very happy upon hearing his unwanted son-in-law is Miguel de Guzmán, coincidentally the very one intended for Cecilia. All rejoice and seek Servando, who has already gone to Pozuelo. Esteban is the mysterious friend awaited so many years. Thus, the three of them will go to Pozuelo the next day.

Act two, in Servando's house, features a large portrait of a woman covered with a black veil, with another portrait of Servando as a young man. Miguel, entering cautiously, informs Gregoria he plans to bring his wife to win over his father, without revealing who she is. Cecilia will pose as the reader-companion Servando is expecting, since his eyes are so bad. Miguel leaves Cecilia to approach Servando, who refuses her services; he will not allow a woman in the house; Gregoria is old, therefore sexless. Cecilia convinces him to try until a male reader is found. Servando, always unhappy and rude, discusses his son and how evil all women are. Cecilia offers to sing and play for him, as well as read, at which the old man becomes interested.

With Miguel anxious to know how things are going, Cecilia follows her father's instructions; offstage she sings the aria "La calumnia" (The Slander), to Servando's dismay; he gazes at the portrait of his late wife in sadness, reminiscing about her last days. As he prepares for the yearly ritual appointment, Esteban arrives (appearing for the first time in thirty years). After a little hesitation the men embrace, recalling the last time they saw each other. Servando returned from a trip, thirty years before, to discover a man in his bedroom speaking words of love to his wife, Elvira. The man fled, and she would not reveal his name, clutching the child in her arms, which prevented Servando from killing her. Esteban confesses it

The Last Plays

was he, but that Elvira had rejected his advances. Convinced he is telling the truth, Servando unveils the portrait, then makes Esteban kneel with him to ask her forgiveness. This done, Servando brings out two pistols and challenges Esteban to a duel. The latter refuses, alleging he has a daughter. Servando reminds him he had a son when Esteban dishonored him. Leave his house, then, says Servando; his doubts are cleared up now; Miguel is his son and he wants to see him, but instead Cecilia enters to read him a tale about a somber house, a man's son, and his emancipation; Miguel then appears and tells the rest. Servando, humanized again, eventually forgives Esteban. The mystery surrounding the portrait of Elvira is well kept until a repentant old man confronts his friend, as forced by the circumstances. The only way to prove the lady's innocence, once doubt was cast on her honor, was to arrange the marriage of Miguel and Cecilia, thereby showing Servando they could not be half-brother-and-sister. Nicholson Adams classifies this play as dull; other critics have neglected it.

VI   Un grano de arena (*A Grain of Sand*)

Un grano de arena, the last play of García Gutiérrez, is a three-act comedy, in verse, performed at the Comedia Theater on December 14, 1880, and published by Rodríguez the same year. In Don Diego's house in Alcalá, Concha inquires of Antonio, a servant, where has he been. After some hesitation he tells her that Isidoro, his master, sent him to Pastrana on an errand. It seems that he once loved a girl who dominated his life for three years, but no longer. Antonio states she is about to die, but he could find no trace of her. Concha reveals that a tearful, veiled woman brought a letter for Don Diego and, in his absence, she told his wife Marta, who also cried. This is interpreted to mean that their marriage is not going well. César, a twelve-year-old child, appears, calling for Concha; he wants to practice shooting with Antonio.

Gaspar and Isidoro discuss a certain debt the latter owes, and whether he still courts Marta, Diego's wife, Isidoro's former sweetheart. Isidoro loves her and wants revenge; Gaspar is likewise vengeful because Diego jilted his daughter Elvira. Diego is due soon, and they will return to Madrid the same day; Isidoro lives in the same building. Antonio runs out, pursued by César with a pistol. Marta orders the child to surrender the dangerous weapon and, to the boy's shame, Antonio shows him it was not properly loaded. Isidoro asks Antonio about his visit to Pastrana; no trace was found of the woman or her child. Later Isidoro tells Marta that her husband has a second child by another woman (Diego, older than Marta, already had César). She wants to see for herself whether Diego is unfaithful to her. When he arrives comments are made about Marta looking sad; she saw a newborn child abandoned by the river. From their conversation it is gathered that Gaspar has returned from France where he had fled when accused of passing counterfeit money; now he wants to retrieve his daughter. Isidoro has initiated his vengeance by making Marta jealous; Gaspar, who wants to make Diego's life miserable through his wife, promises Isidoro to forget his debt if they succeed. The latter affirms he will resort to a fake suicide if necessary. Concha brings news that the lifeless body of a woman has been found by the river, and Isidoro runs to investigate; Gaspar is used to seeing such things in Paris.

Act two takes place in Madrid. As César studies in his father's den, Isidoro enters, seeking Diego, who is not in. He inquires to make sure Marta was told about the other woman. From the conversation between César and Marta we learn she is his stepmother, not a pleasant experience. Marta ponders about the dead woman in the river, concluding she must be Elvira, and that the child is Diego's son. She gives Antonio a letter for Isidoro. When her husband returns, he informs her that they have another son; Marta finds this to be in very poor taste. Angrily, she tells him what she thinks of his illicit affair. Surprised, Diego shows her a letter to clear things up. Marta changes considerably after reading to herself the contents beginning with the words "my second father," and decides to take in the child found by the river. Gaspar and Isidoro see their disruptive plan disintegrating; Marta attempts to retrieve her letter to Isidoro, who refuses to return it.

In the third act Concha informs Antonio that she has been dismissed because she told Marta about something that was Diego's business. Meanwhile, Antonio counts on her to let Isidoro in when her master goes to his club. Marta resents her husband's departure, which he says is necessary. She knows Elvira went to see him and left him a paper. Since Concha had told Marta, Diego did not go to see Elvira, so his wife would not feel betrayed; if he had gone, perhaps the girl would not have committed suicide. Gaspar must be told. César, reconciled with Marta, stays home to defend the women, but soon goes upstairs to see Isidoro's weapons, and Concha leaves the door ajar. Isidoro surprises Marta, alleging he is there to ask her forgiveness, then stages his threat of suicide. She agrees to forgive him; he returns her letter and leaves. As Gaspar comes to see Diego, César rushes in, saying that Isidoro's place is a mess. César found a letter to his mother (dead for some time) next to some gunpowder and a pistol; Isidoro walked in, very pale, and took the weapon. Marta sends the child to sleep, but Gaspar is curious. Marta says she is going to check on Isidoro, but that her husband's honor is safe. Diego arrives, telling Gaspar that Elvira was seeing another man, the reason he left her. A letter from her explains how the other man won her over: by faking suicide. Gaspar cautions Diego that Isidoro must be the man, revealing that Marta has gone to his apartment. As Diego is planning to take justice into his own hands, Marta enters with word that Isidoro has shot himself. Gaspar tries to explain he is an expert on such things, but César confesses he had gone to Isidoro's place without Marta's consent, and because he was ridiculed earlier in Alcalá, he had loaded Isidoro's pistol right. Diego stops the boy from saying more, Marta screams, and Gaspar falls to his knees, exclaiming that now he believes in God. Adams dislikes this last play, finding it unworthy of the author of *El trovador*.

Via a résumé of García Gutiérrez's plays in chronological order, a series of traits and progressions can be perceived. Space does not permit detailed commentary on the outstanding characteristics found in each play as related to others, since at times they are part of a whole that does not hinge on them. Their wide range includes humorous situations, or even a single commentary within a drama, not intended to relieve tension but appropriate to the person involved, making the audience aware that not everyone knows about the problems others have or is concerned about them. The defense of the weak and of victims of injustice is patent in many ways in the plays of García Gutiérrez, one being the intervention of a person of humble origin or low social status. Examples of this are Braulia in *Magdalena*, Azamor in *Zaida* (not merely a servant, but only fifteen years old), Catalina in *El caballero de industria*, the nurse in *Doña Urraca de Castilla*, and others. A strange compromise is Simón of *Los desposorios de Inés*, a servant in his one-time lover's house, who voices his opinion, acts when necessary, but is denied recognition as father of Inés. In contrast we find young people of noble birth, or living below their station, who sense they belong to a higher sphere or yearn for something better, unaware of their true situation on both counts; examples include Manrique in *El trovador*, his counterpart Manuel in the parody *Los hijos del tío Tronera*, Ferrando in *El page*, and others. Strong women abound: Rosa of *Los millonarios*, Ana of *El caballero de industria*, Ana of *Las cañas se vuelven lanzas*, Francisca of *Nobleza obliga*, María also of *Nobleza obliga*, heroic as María Pacheco of *La mujer valerosa* and the María of *Venganza catalana*, and more. In spite of Ferrer del Río's observation that all fathers are kind and loving, Don Ferriz of *El rey monge*, Fiesco of *Simón Bocanegra*, Gircón of *Venganza catalana*, and others are unforgiving with their daughters' lovers in each case; they seem to miss the fact that their daughters were not seduced; whatever relationship they had with the man they loved was voluntary, but no less a source of shame and sorrow for each father.

Other constants are the use of certain names: Inés, Adela, Elvira, María, usually with something in common each time. The Facundos of several plays are also similar; illegitimate children left in infancy in the custody of their father; characters invented or created to develop a love story within a historic play. A challenge or demand for restoration of honor, justified or not, may easily turn into a duel, regardless of the situation and social status of the people involved, or the times in which the play takes place. The honor problem is also hinted at, carried out in different ways, or turned into a joust in medieval times. Not so unusual either in García Gutiérrez's times or in centuries past, we find this situation in too many plays to list them all.

Assumed identity and subterfuge are used in true mystery fashion in comedies of intrigue as well as in dramas dealing with undercover activities, political or private resentments, running the gamut from *El trovador* to *Un grano de arena*, the last play of García Gutiérrez. These recurring traits also involve a variation (not necessarily a progression) of a character. The glaring similarity of *El caballero de industria* and *Los millonarios* is seen not only in the subject but in each type, who in turn has a counterpart in other García Gutiérrez plays if one takes the trouble to seek them out. López Funes observes that *Simón Bocanegra* is the higher expression of *El rey monge*, and *Juan Lorenzo* is superior to *El Encubierto de Valencia*, opening another avenue for a comparative study of García Gutiérrez's plays of different epochs. These examples are by no means exhaustive, suggesting that there is enough material for additional books on García Gutiérrez. Whether drawing from history and forging his own story from a given standpoint, or depicting a slice of life he may have experienced, two things stand out in his theater: a real concern for emotions and how they affect a human being and those around him, and a sense of the theatrical that can be called innate. One reason for the scant criticism extant on the works of our author is the fact that the collection compiled in his honor includes only nineteen plays, omitting some of his best, perhaps in order to include a variety; thus other plays, as well as many written after the homage volume, dated 1866, received little or no publicity, as they were printed separately, one by one.

CHAPTER 7

Zarzuelas

I *The Genre*

NO specific label exists that accurately designates in English what a *zarzuela* is. Translated as musical comedy or operetta, it would imply a type of frivolous theater with music which recalls any such piece the reader might have seen, but equates this idea with something totally foreign. There are conjectures and statements about the origin of the word, references to early works that contained some of the elements of the *zarzuela*, and studies considered authoritative which trace influences in the *zarzuela* music, especially the Italian. A Spaniard knows instinctively what he is enjoying: a *zarzuela grande* (grand zarzuela), *zarzuela*, or *género chico* (short or lesser *zarzuela*). The music, the dialogue, the setting, denominate the work. The *zarzuela*, whatever its period of formation or its structure, reached maturity and greatest splendor in the period from the second half of the nineteenth century to 1936, when the Spanish Civil War destroyed or paralyzed so many things in the country. No subsequent *zarzuela* revival has been noted among many artistic endeavors, and even attempts by some already reknowned composers have not sufficed to stimulate the genre in the postwar period.

Zarzuela grande implies an operatic quality; plain *zarzuela* is usually two or three acts long, and alternates music and dialogue, leaving the exposure of important facts or feelings to arias (*romanzas* in Spanish) or duets. The chorus may intervene either for commentary, for questions and answers, or as part of the plot. There is always a comic character, reminiscent of the *gracioso* (funny or humorous type) of the *comedia*, but he is not (as in earlier times) necessarily a servant; he can be a minor character, a townsperson, an old man, a waiter, or a peasant. A comic role is also entrusted to a woman, usually related to the man: his wife or sweetheart, a maid, or a neighbor. The text elicits the music according to the sensibility of the composer, in collaboration with the librettist, as they determine what merits a *romanza* or a duet; what characters, if any, receive an identifying theme, or when one should be used as a given portion of an earlier episode is repeated, either vocally or by an instrument. Although some *zarzuelas* have an overture setting the mood, it is common for the overture to be composed of several themes later heard in *romanzas* and salient points of the *zarzuela*.

The *género chico* tends to deal with everyday life, especially in Madrid neighborhoods, portraying characters whose special appeal is to those who see their own street or sector of the city portrayed on stage. The music tends to be more a means of enhancing the spoken parts or complementing them with singing. The popularity of this very Spanish form of entertainment, with its endless variety of subjects, accounts for the unfortunate fact that an excessively small orchestra was ordinarily used, which could not do justice to the beauty of the music some composers poured into an inspired libretto. *Zarzuela* companies, by tradition, had the difficult task of performing a different work every day, and often two in the same evening during the theatrical season. A tenor or a *tiple* (soprano) singing a leading role one night in one *zarzuela* might sing a secondary role in another; a good baritone might have to settle for a secondary role in many such pieces, only to shine in others as the main character. Within the same *zarzuela* there may be two good roles suitable for the same voice, making it hard for singers to learn both without becoming confused on stage. In recent years more attention has been paid to producing *zarzuelas* with large orchestras and augmented choruses. Except for the ones set in modern times, period costumes lend added attractiveness to the whole. The *zarzuelas* recorded by internationally acclaimed Spanish singers usually lack the spoken dialogue; thus they are beautiful, but incomplete.

A peculiarity worth noting is that rarely is there a part for a mezzo-soprano or contralto in most *zarzuelas*, the tendency being to have two sopranos, one dramatic and one lyric (or with a light voice), when there are two important women's roles. Leading roles for men are not necessarily reserved for tenors; a baritone may not be the hero or the one who ends up with the girl, but often he is the most important character in a *zarzuela*, and sometimes the star, relegating the tenor to a comic or secondary role. In all *zarzuelas* there are minor scenes, relevant to the plot only in a limited way, providing an entertaining link as they are sung, and full of movement because of the chorus. The dress identifies the trade of the people involved, aided at times by props, and their action of the moment is sung, whether complaining about their work, the weather, enjoying their rest, looking forward to the next moment or setting the mood for coming events. These scenes delight the spectator visually and auditorially in a way a straight play cannot achieve. In the case of Antonio García Gutiérrez, his knack for plasticity is an asset, as he is truly able to bring to life the scenes he pictures in his mind via the contribution of words, singing, and movement.

Emilio Arrieta, who composed the music for most of the librettos of García Gutiérrez, tended to be dramatic and brilliant in his best-known *zarzuelas grandes* or operas. Francisco Asenjo Barbieri had a light touch many call Italianate; he has also been accused of rigging and exploiting his mother's last name in order to appear Italian: Barbieri was the surname he preferred to Asenjo, equally uncommon. The remaining composers who put music to other García Gutiérrez plots are less well known. In chronological order of either performance, or date of publication (sometimes difficult to ascertain), García Gutiérrez's list of *zarzuelas* follows, with some discussion of sample plots: *La espada de Bernardo* (Bernard's Sword), 1853; *El hijo de familia o el lancero voluntario* (The Playboy or the Voluntary Lancer), 1853; *El grumete* (The Ship-boy), 1853; *La cacería real* (The Royal Hunt), 1853; *Un día de reinado* (One Day of Reign), 1854; *Azon Visconti*, 1858; *El robo de las sabinas* (The Rape of the Sabines), 1859; *Cegar para ver* (To Become Blind in Order to See), 1860; *Llamada y tropa* (Call and Troop), 1861; *Dos coronas* (Two Crowns), 1861; *Galáni de noche* (Night Suitor), 1862; *La tabernera de Londres* (The Tavern Keeper Girl of London), 1862; *La vuelta del corsario* (The Return of the Pirate), 1863; and *El capitán negrero* (The Slave Dealer Captain), 1865.

II *The* Zarzuela *Librettos of García Gutiérrez*

La espada de Bernardo (Bernard's Sword), performed in the Circo Theater January 14, 1853, was published by D. F. R. del Castillo, Madrid, in the same year. This first *zarzuela* libretto by García Gutiérrez, with music by Francisco Asenjo Barbieri, presents an intrigue not unlike the cape and sword plays of the seventeenth century, but with a new twist. Bernardo, the terror of Madrid, is in reality a coward who feigns losing his sword (which does not cut) and falling dead. Eventually he falls prey to his own bragging, and ends up in jail, ready to be executed for a murder: his own. Once things are straightened out and he is exposed, all ends well.

The language is mostly in jest, except for two characters and specific scenes. Although the plot is of no major consequence, the ambience of a Calderón play is maintained, updated somewhat to García Gutiérrez's times by the language, and the *gracioso* is given a nice part to act and sing. Some scenes are very intricate and difficult for the singers, with discussions that are verisimilar and spontaneous-like dialogues with several people taking part (including some in hiding), as well as comments and asides to different persons. Groups do not necessarily constitute a trio or quartet or answer to any such label. The third act, for instance, begins with Bernardo in jail and a chorus of prisoners playing cards, ending in a brawl which he stops solely with his fame as a "killer." Indicative of the festive mood of the piece, not overdone or broad in its humor, at one point three old ladies come to their doors or windows with oil lamps to see what the commotion in the street is all about: the ladies are played by men.

El hijo de familia o el lancero voluntario (The Playboy or the Voluntary Lancer) was performed in December of 1853 in the Circo Theater. Printed by Muñoz, Madrid, 1854, it is allegedly a translation from the French, but no details are given. Julián visits a military post seeking his friend Alberto, a playboy whose father has just cut off his income. Alberto is attracted to Paulina, whom he believes to be a peasant but is in reality a widowed aristocrat whose aunt, a countess, plans to marry her to the post colonel, rather well known for his temper; Paulina wanted to observe him before meeting him. The wedding is being planned by the Colonel's sister, three times a widow of military men and, like her brother, very bossy. The Colonel proves to be fair when he refuses a contracted marriage. Alberto is replaced by a paid substitute in the army and returns to his banker father. It is not clear whether he ends up with Paulina or not.

The intricate misunderstandings and deceits, with mixing of ranks, are very amusingly wrought, with the chorus of lancers and their trumpeteer livening up the proceedings, especially at the beginning and the end. Adding to the confusion, the mess-hall keeper goes along with Alberto by saying, to avoid military reprimand, that he spent the night with her; even when her fiancé and others defend her honor she insists on her cover-up, denying she is innocent or honest. The only indication given in this piece as to the composer is an initial O, and a penciled question as to whether it is Cristóbal Oudrid.

El grumete (The Ship-boy) was performed in the Circo Theater in June 1853 and printed by Rodríguez in 1856, the composer being Emilio Arrieta.[1] It takes place in a small town on the Cantabrian coast of Spain at the beginning of the nineteenth century. A prelude expressing dawn is completed by a chorus of peasants bringing baskets of flowers and fruits to Luisa, who is about to be married. She thanks them in song, but from conversations with her parents and Antón, her fiancé, we gather she yearns for someone else. Serafín (played by a girl) has jumped ship to see Luisa; she tells him of her impending wedding and their parting duet ends with an embrace. He will speak to her father, Pascual. Antón and Luisa converse and she expresses her true feelings; Serafín returns and confronts Antón. The boy's uncle, Tomás, a pirate, comes to retrieve him, attempting to dissuade him of his plans. Later Tomás speaks with Luisa's parents, deciding that the best thing is to separate the youngsters. In a duet Pascual and Tomás discuss Serafín's good and bad points, with the boy avidly defended by his uncle. Luisa and Serafín have no choice but to part, but as Tomás seeks his nephew, he meets the girl, whom he finds enchanting. A trío follows in which he agrees to the wedding. Antón, rejected and sad, leaves. The pirate returns to his ship with Pascual for treasures that belong to Serafín. A final chorus with peasants and sailors marks the wedding festivities.

The dialogue is brisk, with a rustic tone that is blunt at times but quite right for the station in life of the people depicted. Antón seems a bit course, but one feels sorry for him when he loses Luisa. The love and despair expressed by the young boy and girl, when faced with the cold reasoning of their elders, have a poignant quality. Tomás emerges as a strong man, used to the rough life of the sea, but wondering what having a safe harbor would be like. He returns to brave the ocean and other buccaneers, but now having a place to rest on land. According to Antonio Palau y Dulcet's *Manual del librero Hispanoamericano* (The Spanish American Bookseller's

Manual) Justo Moro made a shortened version of Arrieta's score in 1853. The date does not indicate whether it was that of publication or of the revision.

La cacería real (The Royal Hunt) was also performed in the Circo Theater in 1853 and published by Rodríguez in 1854, in Madrid; Arrieta is the composer. Taken in part from an unidentified play by Collé it occurs in the Pardo, a royal palace some distance from Madrid, in 1704. Two choruses of noblemen comment upon a trip the King plans to take and how Prince Cariñano has fallen in the ill graces of the King. The Marquis of Villena reassures the Prince of his innocence, to the relief of the chorus. In a duet, however, the Marquis reveals his poor opinion of the Prince, while the latter conveys how impressed he is by the strict honor code of the Spaniards. The King, who is single, tries to learn more about the Prince and his intentions toward a young lady whom evidently both like; it is Margarita, who pleads that her reputation is ruined (she does not state by whom) without cause, and everyone except her boyfriend avoids her. During a hunt the different parties are separated by a storm, and the King, concealing his identity, takes refuge in the house of a forest guard, whose son Pascual is Margarita's boyfriend. She later arrives, begging for shelter, since her own family has rejected her. The stranger responsible for her dishonor is the King, but no one tells the family. During supper the King realizes how honorable his subjects are and, as the group of noblemen and villagers, alerted by Pascual, enter the house, the Prince is put to shame. The King joins Margarita and Pascual, promising to rid the country of traitors, since the honor of Spain is also his honor. The language, as in other *zarzuelas*, is sharp in the comments made by the Marquis and Pascual, but very proper in the women's roles.

Un día de reinado (A Day of Reign) is a translation and adaptation done with the aid of D. L. Olona of a play by Scribe and St. Georges. Performed at the Circo Theater in February of 1854, it was published the same year by Rodríguez. There is no indication as to the composer. The action begins in Calais and ends in Brighton. Marcelo and Rufina love each other but cannot marry until one of them makes some money. He has the opportunity to marry a tavern keeper from Calais who is going to take charge of the tavern her widowed uncle owns in Brighton. Rufina agrees to pose as a lady at the request of a Count, being for a time unsure what her role is; the others are also confused. Is she posing as a noble lady or is she the King's wife disguised as a seamstress? The plot was a device to divert attention from Charles II, who, while soldiers retain the alleged queen, enters London with his true wife and wins the British crown. Rufina receives her reward, so Marcelo and she can marry. The sung parts are in verse, the dialogue in prose. All roles include funny remarks, especially those of the working class, either when gossiping or when they find themselves in a compromising situation.

Azon Visconti, with music by Emilio Arrieta, was performed at the Zarzuela Theater the same year it was published by Rodríguez, in Madrid (1858). It takes place around Milan in the year 1314. During the siege of Milan Lorenzo, a traitor, is caught in a plot to overthrow Prince Azon Visconti. He is unaware that his daughter Laura supports the Prince, and his other daughter, Angelica, is the Prince's lady love. Count Oswaldo aids Prince Azon, attempting to dissuade him from his love for a villager (Angelica), who proves to be Oswaldo's long-lost sister, saved by Lorenzo during the sack of a place in Tuscany. Love and honor triumph at the end as Lorenzo promises his daughter Laura to mend his ways, and the Prince marries Angelica.

Assorted choruses and solos, aside from the many difficult and exposed situations sung by Beppo, a spy in disguise, underscore the intrigue. The beginning of the third act provides a complete idea of what an intricate endeavor it is to produce this kind of theater: for a scant two pages of script and action as well as singing, ended by a noontime bell, the scene represents a square in Milan being fortified; soldiers pound iron on anvils, sharpening swords and spears; some women draw wine from a cask while others serve it to the men; other women gather arrows in bunches, while veteran soldiers teach recruits who do not quite grasp the art of wielding a sword, and elsewhere soldiers practice archery. The fact that García Gutiérrez refers to "Italy" in 1314 may be criticized by some, just as he was criticized for referring to the feats of the army in *Venganza catalana* (Catalan Revenge) as a victory for Spain, when neither country yet had such a name in medieval times. This may have been done in the nineteenth century not as an anachronism, but as a means to identify the geographical location for the theatergoer, who is under no obligation to be erudite.

El robo de las sabinas (The Rape of the Sabines) was performed at the Zarzuela Theater in February of 1859, and published in Madrid by Ducazcal the same year. The music was composed by

Francisco Asenjo Barbieri. In an unidentified place at the end of the seventeenth century, we find Countess Aurora, who, on her way to meet her husband-to-be, a duke, stops at an inn with her ladies, all past their prime (over fifty years of age). There the Duke, in disguise, carries out her abduction, taking everyone to his nearby castle. He is amazed at Aurora's acceptance of his wooing, until it is discovered that his mother had warned her about her son's devious ways, so Aurora has played along to teach him a lesson. Among the amusing scenes in the *zarzuela*, the end of the first act depicts the ladies running in all directions and being grabbed, with obvious disgust, by the young gentlemen the Duke brought with him, while the Seneschal faints in the arms of the innkeeper's daughter. Another occurs when the innkeeper, seeking help, succeeds in recruiting a grand total of four soldiers (of the 2,000 needed to raid the castle) but obtains twenty trumpeteers and all the drummers of the territory.

III Zarzuelas *of the 1860s*

Cegar para ver (To Become Blind in Order to See) was published by Rodríguez in Madrid in 1860 and performed at the Circo Theater (no date given). Salvador Ruiz composed the music for this *zarzuela*. Occurring in Calahorra, in the province of Logroño, in 1814, it features a duet between Juana and Carlos which informs the audience that Blas, her father, is forcing her to marry Hipólito, an older man blinded by a bullet in the war, who will leave his fortune to father and daughter. Hipólito appears, cured (a fact he conceals until, by observing everyone's behavior, he is convinced that only the father wants the wedding). He tests the young couple's feelings in a less than subtle way, forcing them to make gestures and silent comments he can very well see. The father is disappointed and fights to the end, but Hipólito saw him lift a chair and menace his daughter while Juana said her free will was not being forced in any way. The young people will wed.

Llamada y tropa (Call and Troop). Performed in March of 1861 at the Circo Theater, it was published by González in Madrid in the same year. Emilio Arrieta composed the music. It takes place in a student boarding house in Salamanca in the mid-1830s. Brígida takes her daughter out of convent school to marry her to Sotero, an old and ugly man the girl rejects. Of three suitors that visited her window grill at the school, eventually she rejects the first one for being poor, and the second for following the dangerous profession of army captain, while the third rejects *her* for being too cunning. A chorus of students, the captain (always accompanied by soldiers and music), and the conversations held with asides, added to the comments of the three suitors in hiding, make the comic intrigue more lively. The copy of this *zarzuela* script I consulted is marked on every page, obviously having been used for a performance. Names of actors, cuts, reminders, and other notes are penciled in.

Dos coronas (Two Crowns), adapted from the French, was performed at the Circo Theater in December 1861 and published in Madrid by Rodríguez the same year. It takes place in Hanover in 1711 and 1714; Arrieta composed the music. Two girls raised in a convent part upon graduation, exchanging the crown each earned, one for excellence in voice, the other in history. With her voice teacher the singer goes to Italy, and years later she is reunited with her friend in Hanover, via a message tied to her crown. She prefers to visit her friend to allow the advances of a suitor they both had in the convent. The friend proves to be the Queen of England and the former suitor is her husband, the King. The singer returns to Italy to avoid trouble; her own cares vanish when she is on stage. Scenes worth mentioning include, for instance, the opening chorus of girls rejecting their music lesson, and later attempts to hide a young man who has jumped over the convent walls. The second act opens with a chorus of Egyptians being scolded by the conductor because they are bad singers, bad actors, and thoroughly dull; then he demonstrates the proper way of singing, which they imitate none too well.

Galán de noche (Night Suitor), with music by José Inzenga, was published by Rodríguez (Madrid, 1862) and performed at the Circo Theater, with no date available. Also a translation without details as to origin, it takes place in Italy. With bold and extravagant behavior, using a series of disguises and intrigues, Count Grimani woos a lady. Finally victorious, he will be her daytime suitor as well. A curious scene of the type that makes *zarzuela* such a different form of theater, is the opening of the play with a chorus of carriage drivers drinking and talking about their work until the innkeeper comes in and gives out their assignments. One of the characters, for lack of anyone to talk to, tells the audience his story.

La tabernera de Londres (The Tavern-keeper Girl of London), with score by Arrieta, was performed at the Circo Theater on November 14, 1862, and published the same year in Madrid by Rodríguez. A translation from the French author Scribe, it is an intrigue of love, religion, and politics set in 1553, with a noblewoman disguised as the tavern keeper. All ends with the proclamation of Mary Tudor as Queen, and Jane Grey, fourth wife of Henry VIII, being deposed.

La vuelta del corsario (The Return of the Pirate), performed at the Circo Theater in November 1863 and published the same year in Madrid by Rodríguez, is the second part of *El grumete* (The Shipboy), the music also by Arrieta. This sequel came ten years after the first part. At harvest time a chorus takes baskets of grapes to be crushed, and Luisa receives the men returning from a partridge hunt. Antón complains that Serafín chases every girl, including Antón's bride-to-be. Luisa, hurt by her husband Serafín's behavior, reminds him when he leaves for the tavern that they have a baby. (Serafín is played by a girl, as was also done in the *Grumete*). Antón suggests that Luisa try to make her husband jealous so he will mend his ways. This is accomplished by having people watch the deceit and singing their comments, intermingled with a duet by Luisa and Antón. When the couple are reconciled, Tomás asks for a nephew, since the baby they already have is a girl, not much good for the sea. The *zarzuela* ends with the harvester's return and the pirate's preparing to sail again.

El capitán negrero (The Slave-dealer Captain) is the last *zarzuela* script of García Gutiérrez. Published in Madrid by Rodríguez in 1865, it was performed at the Zarzuela Theater in December of that year. Arrieta composed the music for this work also. This play takes place in a harbor in the United States where Palmer, a Negro slave dealer, readying the *Alondra* for sailing, recalls how he wounded Enrique, twin brother of his girl, Paulina, because the young man prevented him from chasing a girl in Baltimore. Paulina has received a letter from a friend of her brother's informing her of the situation; she knows that if Enrique does not report to the warship *Ariel* his career may be ruined, so she decides to take his place. Elena goes to care for the wounded boy to the dismay of her boyfriend Jonatás, who is approached by Palmer about a post in his ship, resulting in a series of incidents that cause the *Ariel* to pursue the *Alondra*. Paulina has troubles on board since one of the officers, Rock, is a suitor, and Palmer suspects that the twin has taken Enrique's place, a fact eventually discovered. To avoid further trouble, since Palmer tries to implicate others in his wrongdoings, he provokes a fire aboard the *Ariel*, and "saves" most of the crew. People from both ships are stranded on faraway shores while Palmer, now a plantation man, awaits pardon for his devious ways, having saved the crew of the *Ariel*. Paulina is seemingly about to wed Rock, but only to spite Palmer and make him return to an honest life-style. In the end she will marry Palmer, on condition that the slaves he has recruited be set free. She had also spent her savings to replace the *Ariel*.

The opening of act three shows Jonatás in charge of teaching a group of Negro slaves the alphabet, which they have learned, after a year, up to the letter K; but they can make combinations of letters meaning *food, drink, sleep,* and *loaf*. Very striking in a serious way is the fire Palmer provokes in the storeroom of the ship in the second act. At the end of the play there is a note explaining in detail the set for the second act.

In many of these librettos there is a list of characters with the names of the actors and singers who performed each *zarzuela*. Several names recur in a good number of them, indicating an artist most suitable for certain roles and perhaps parts written for him; such is the case of the comic roles performed by Vicente Caltañazor, who appears in nine of the fourteen *zarzuelas*. The same is true of another actor, Francisco Calvet. Hartzenbusch praises García Gutiérrez for his many *zarzuelas*, five of which were included in the collection of selected works. As it was being printed, *El capitán negrero* was being performed for the first time in Madrid, simultaneously with his play *Juan Lorenzo*. Some characters and different traits observed in the plays of García Gutiérrez are also easily detected as being present in his *zarzuelas*.

CHAPTER 8

Spain and Giuseppe Verdi

I Victor Hugo and Giuseppe Verdi

SPAIN and Spanish themes, real or fictitious, have perennially fascinated foreign artists, especially writers and musicians. Giuseppe Verdi and Victor Hugo are two fine examples of this. Each was captivated by the Spanish charm in a different way, and by coincidence their artistry flourished with a strong Spanish element they felt, whether they recognized it or were unaware of it, as in the case of Verdi. He had considered *Cromwell*, by Victor Hugo, as a possible libretto for an opera, but rejected it because it contained too many characters. However, this play led Verdi to read others by the same author, one of them *Hernani*, which became an opera in 1843. I regret that editorial limitations prevent the inclusion of a study of this play, and of Angel de Saavedra's *Don Alvaro o la fuerza del sino* (Don Alvaro or the Power of Fate), and their operatic versions as adapted by Verdi. These operas present many points of contact with García Gutiérrez's *El trovador* and *Simón Bocanegra*, also honored by Verdi with his music. A number of other operas by the same and other composers contain many Spanish elements, some of them traceable in an unexpected way. If Antonio García Gutiérrez imitated or copied others, as some critics indicate, the amount and quality of such emulation has to be studied. In this aspect we might point out the use of alternating verse and prose, as well as music, in his *Trovador*, as Angel de Saavedra had done in his *Don Alvaro o la fuerza del sino*. García Gutiérrez also titled each act, as Victor Hugo did in *Hernani*. These are two good examples of his gathering ideas he could put to use to enhance his own creation, which is not plagiarism. Other details can be contrasted with *Hernani* as a play and the Spanish elements it contains. The live model for the protagonist was Juan Martín "El Empeci nado," a *guerrillero* dedicated to free Spain of the French invaders. Another character on which Hernani is based is Pedro of *El tejedor de Segovia* (The Weaver from Segovia), a creation of Juan Ruiz de Alarcón, author of *La verdad sospechosa* (Suspicious Truth) used by Corneille to write his *Menteur* (Liar), which in turn served as inspiration to Molière to write his *Misanthrope*.[1] Guillaume Huzsar, as mentioned in chapter 1, elaborates considerably on this point.

II Antonio García Gutiérrez's El trovador

In January of 1850, Verdi asked his librettist Cammarano to locate the text of *El trovador*. Not satisfied with the resulting script, both men went to work on it. Verdi seems to have been very particular about some of the operas for which he composed music, especially when, as in the case of *El trovador*, he wanted to do it although he had not been commissioned to prepare an opera for any given theater. The gypsy was a fascinating character and he wanted an outstanding mezzo for the part. The original play had to be changed to adjust the story to the different type of theater opera is, eliminating minor characters, scenes, and some details in order to maintain the musical pace uninterrupted. The play, however, was so rich and powerful that any cut would spoil the whole, a clear sign that Verdi worked on it for artistic reasons beyond being interested in the musical possibilities of the plot and was involved in the story as much as in the superb theater created by García Gutiérrez.

For those who have seen the opera and have read the play in detail, it is not difficult to notice that the famous "anvil chorus" of the second act is a most happy addition: instead of presenting Azucena alone with Manrique next to the fire in the same spot where her mother was burned, Verdi and his librettist place the scene in the gypsy camp, adding the color and movement of gypsy dress and trade. However, in such scenes as the beginning of the first act; the several actions taking place outside the convent, while the audience observed Leonor professing as a nun inside; the dramatic duo of Leonor and Manrique, who are unable to communicate, with one inside and the other outside the tower, intermingled with the choir of monks intoning the *Miserere*, are scenes taken literally from the play. Those who criticize the libretto have no idea of what a bad English translation filtered through Italian from Spanish can do to any play. Résumés of plots are usually faulty if brief, and confusing if long; it is a pity the operagoer cannot be made to read the entire libretto in the original beforehand.

The *Trovador*, written by a youth, struck Verdi's artistic fiber with tremendous force; born the same year as García Gutiérrez, Verdi was in his late thirties when he finished the music for this opera. Cammarano had died in the meantime, so part of the third act and all the fourth were completed by Leone Emanuele Bardare. Any shortcomings in the text Verdi smoothed over with his unsurpassed music. There are those who insist Verdi was experimenting with voice effects, attempting to get away from recitative, aria, duo, and crowd scene. This only the composer could explain. Whether he was experimenting or obeying his creative impulse within the limitations or guidelines of a drama, he composed beautiful ensembles and demanding arias and duos for every voice, not always making the tenor a hero or the baritone a villain. In this particular case the real villain is, in the end, the gypsy. The Count of Luna is moved by love and jealousy, and is hurt by rejection; his crime of executing his brother, unknowingly, is the fulfillment of Azucena's long-term desire for revenge. According to William Weaver, some of the music composed for Azucena was inspired by the recent death of Verdi's mother. Aside from his interest in finding a suitable singer for the role of Azucena, and the death of Cammarano, the composition of *Il Trovatore* was interrupted by the commissioning of *La traviata*, which Verdi composed in about a year and later revised and improved.

Weaver, George Martin, and others contend that some of the background material being narrated, rather than performed on stage, makes for holes in the story. The original play did not suffer in that way because the audience understood every word, which is not so easy when being sung in another language. Martin, in his evaluation of this opera, compares it to others by Verdi. Although his evaluation is favorable and he stresses the emotional effects of the opera, he does not fully realize that what Verdi often did was to follow the theatrical piece as something upon which he could not improve, an example being the last act.

III *Antonio García Gutiérrez's* Simón Bocanegra

It may be puzzling that Verdi would use the play on Simón Bocanegra by García Gutiérrez instead of looking up the facts in a history book of his native Italy. Perhaps the love intrigue and the long-lost girl added the dimension he wanted, giving a more sentimental aspect to the former pirate who twice became ruler and then died, poisoned. An impossibly long and complicated play in one prologue and four acts was not the easiest thing to reduce to a manageable libretto, as proven by the fact that the opera did not achieve as much success as others by Verdi when first performed, notwithstanding its magnificent score. Twenty-four years later Verdi revised his opera. Seldom performed because of the difficulties it poses, it is, however, well worth waiting for. The résumé of the plot as given in the program is confusing to the point that the spectator might consider leaving the theater with a monumental headache after trying to make some sense out of it, or stay to listen to the music and leave it at that. Such was my case years ago. My first surprise was the beauty of the music as the curtain went up; the second was to discover that no libretto and program were necessary: the action was self-explanatory, with the arias and duos so aptly placed that the whole flowed effortlessly. Once more the mark of two superb artists, dramatist and composer, gifted with a similar genius for the stage, bore fruit. Verdi used traditional voices for his characters, achieving singular beauty, for instance, in Fiesco's lament for the death of his daughter, one of the select pieces for a bass and in the duo between Simón Bocanegra and Gabriel Adorno (baritone and tenor), and the encounter of father and daughter (baritone and soprano).

The opera was first performed in Venice on March 12, 1857, in the Fenice Theater. The librettist was Francesco Maria Piave. The revision was done later by Arrigo Boito, whose new version, performed in the Scala of Milan on March 24, 1881, is the one that exists today. Some changes were made in relation to the earlier opera and to the play; for instance, Simón Bocanegra learns that Amelia (Susana in the play) is his daughter at the Grimaldi palace, not afterwards. The girl is already aware of their relationship when Gabriel Adorno appears, wounded, and she asks forgiveness for him when he accuses Simón of abducting her. Gabriel is kept prisoner. All this takes place in the first act. In the second act Paolo has already poured the poison into Bocanegra's goblet when he tells Fiesco, who rebukes him. In the third act Paolo, taken prisoner, says his vengeance is already taking place. Fiesco disapproves (although he also wants to even the score with Bocanegra), then tells him he has been poisoned when Simón reveals that his daughter is Amelia, thus keeping his word to find her so he can be pardoned by Fiesco. Essentially the events that are retained are: the death of María (Mariana), Fiesco's resentment, Bocanegra proclaimed Dux, his encounter with his daughter, her love and that of Gabriel, the subsequent reconciliation with Fiesco, and Gabriel Adorno's siding with Simón Bocanegra.

Those who say, as does George Martin, that the *Trovador* and *Simón Bocanegra* needed a prologue since so much background material had to be given, fail to see that in both cases the librettists put it precisely where the dramatist had placed it, since that is where they found it. Some of the theatrical effects are also marked or suggested in the play, with great economy of words, from the lighting effects of the prologue and of the last act, to the places where Verdi inserted arias or duos, using monologues or conversations found in the play. The plays and operas briefly discussed here point to a preference of Giuseppe Verdi for things Spanish. *Il Trovatore* has maintained a place of honor in opera houses throughout the world, closely followed by *La forza del destino; Ernani* and *Simón Bocanegra* follow at a distance. Verdi also studied Victor Hugo's *Ruy Blas*, the story of a Spanish valet of the seventeenth century who loves the queen, but Marchetti had already composed an opera on the same subject, and Verdi abandoned the idea. *Le roi s'amuse*[2] lives today as *Rigoletto*, and here the protagonist is a character drawn from a Spanish model; play and opera would not have as much impact were the main character not a misshapen buffoon. According to George Martin *Ernani* and *Rigoletto* were easier to make into librettos because the plays from which they were drawn had more action than narrative, as opposed to *El trovador* and *Simón Bocanegra*. To this we might respond that these plays were written by different men telling different stories. Also, Hugo, drawing from the Spanish, had to be more direct and explicit.

Other more or less Spanish themes that appealed to Verdi are found in his opera *Don Carlo*, based on *Don Carlos*, by Schiller, about the hypothetical life which the unfortunate prince, son of Felipe II and María de Portugal, could have had. *I vespri siciliani*, composed for the Opera of Paris, deals with the French defeat at Palermo, but the libretto was a variation of one written for Donizetti in 1840 about the Spanish occupation of the Low Countries, titled

Il Duca d'Alba.³ *La bataglia di Legnano*, dealing with the defeat of Barbarossa by the Lombards, was censored because Italy was in a similar political situation in 1848, so the plot was changed to the Dutch rebellion of the sixteenth century against the Spaniards, leaving the music intact.

It is puzzling that García Gutiérrez in his *Un cuento de niños* (A Children's Tale), already commented upon, should appear to dislike Verdi's music, considering that the latter chose two of his plays from which to compose operas. His opinion is stated in a more specific way in the second act of the play by grouchy Servando, over seventy years of age.⁴ It seems that García Gutiérrez deplored the loud music of his day, although it was in keeping with the release of emotions of the characters depicted in dramas and novels of the time. García Gutiérrez was more in favor of a restrained elegance and soft tones accompanying quiet desperation and hidden wounds. At the same time, since he has old Esteban and Servando, a bitter man, express those unfavorable opinions, the author's position is not entirely unequivocal, since in no other play have I found similar comments.

CHAPTER 9

Poetry

I *The Entrambasaguas Edition*

IN 1947 Joaquín de Entrambasaguas published the poetry of Antonio García Gutiérrez. He regrets being unsuccessful in his efforts to gather all the poetry of our author, since much material remains unpublished or scattered in publications not available to him. The prologuist lists rare editions such as that of *Un baile en casa de Abrantes* (A Dance in Abrantes's House), describing the copy he consulted, and later includes the text without commentary. It has to be hunted for, like many items in his book, and a very dry account of this piece is found on page lviii. Entrambasaguas tells where poems were first published, following with those not previously printed. Then he expounds his theory concerning the creativity of García Gutiérrez and his evaluation as a poet, taking into account such things as his early readings and education and vogues and tastes of the times, but making sweeping statements, as if the individual were chained to the lyric baggage inherited through the centuries. Appraisal of the poet becomes a mere balance of pros and cons stipulated by the critic, who finds dramatic poetry in García Gutiérrez's nondramatic works and sheer lyricism in excerpts of his plays, as though the poet had no right to let his pen flow directed solely by his inspiration. Agreeing in principle that his dramatic works surpass his lyric poetry, it is somewhat disconcerting to find words such as "contamination" describing dramatic aspects in García Gutiérrez's poetry, or the attribution of "false modesty" to his claim that an editor wanted to publish his poetry (Entrambasaguas fails to take into account the fact that at the time García Gutiérrez was already a famous dramatist).

Entrambasaguas first comments upon the erotic poems, but since they are not presented in an orderly way, and he jumps from one part of the book to another, not even following the progressive order of pagination, it is nearly impossible to find or trace a cohesive pattern, and useless to try to check on a given poem. Given the aesthetic and academic framework in which Entrambasaguas situates each poem, he finds turns and qualities that seem to surprise him, since he is looking at the verses with a critical eye, not with the spontaneity with which a reader who likes poetry approaches a poem. Hence the sonority in one, and delicate sensibility in another, are aided by the meter used.

The epic and heroic tone of some poems the prologuist deems unsatisfactory, and on this count we agree with him. However, those pieces belong to a different sphere, and elicit little emotion from the author, because García Gutiérrez, when following a specific event, can do little more than repeat it or remember it, while the same material has infinitely more possibilities as a dramatic work. Even in the treatment of historic episodes, the dramatic sensitivity of García Gutiérrez seeps through in his use of the language. Entrambasaguas detects a certain biblical flavor in some, and firm and heroic tones in several with a patriotic subject; a certain air reminiscent of the old *romances* (ballads), and an uneven quality in the religious poems, which are contrasted with those of José Zorrilla and Alberto Lista, both of whom surpass García Gutiérrez. However, García Gutiérrez seems to possess a special knack for turning out the right form of expression, and with this comes a certain honesty responsible for a description, a moment, a memory merely written in verse but not necessarily poetic; sometimes he is brief and prosaic. On pages liv and lv of the prologue Entrambasaguas transcribes part of the legend of the ghost of Valladolid, to be noted later.

II *The Text*

The first piece in the text is "Un baile en casa de Abrantes," which I had previously read in the Repullés edition (Madrid, 1834). The scene is set in Don Pablo's bedroom; he is in bed. Tadeo comes to visit him, and Pablo says he has a cold; the night before he went with his wife to a masked ball in Abrantes's house. The lady was besieged by other masked men, and she left him alone for awhile. Pablo ended up in the buffet room, and imbibed until he became so dizzy he went home, weaving through the streets. Daytime came, and with it many bilious and tired faces, among them his wife's, but he does not doubt her fidelity. The poem ends as Tadeo goes on to the Retiro Park for a walk, and Pablo stays in bed.

In verse, the description of the dance, the house, and the lavish buffet is bright and very graphic. So is the subtle irony of the freedom which a costume and an atmosphere of music, food, and drink, give to people, even to very proper women. Pablo lost sight of his wife involuntarily, but it was foolish of him, or at least not very judicious, to leave the ball under the influence of alcohol, leaving his wife unattended.

After a foreword by García Gutiérrez already mentioned in part III of chapter 1 as well as at the beginning of this chapter, twenty-two poems follow. The first, "Las dos rivales" (The Two Rivals), is the tale in five parts of a girl who, dressed in a man's clothing, sadly weeping rides to Jaén, enters a church to pray, and then proceeds to Diego Laínez's house on his wedding day. Passing herself off as a young troubadour, the beautiful blond youth delights everyone but the bridegroom with a song about a young man who wooed two girls at the same time. Someone thinks there is a silver phial of poison in the musician's hand as he proposes a toast for the bride. After all retire, the bride is found dead. Diego hears a moan and pursues a shadow leaning against a wall in its flight. The next day both dead women are taken out of the house, accompanied by an anguished man (Diego) along the Street of the Dead. Everyone is frightened as they pass by. On the road to Porcuna four pines shade the tomb of Inés de Albarracín. The language of García Gutiérrez here has the same force and life found in many of his tragic theatrical passages. The images evoked are so precise one can picture the entire story as if caught in the middle of it. The tomb's being outside sacred grounds means Inés poisoned the other girl and herself, thus committing a crime and then suicide.

"A Cádiz" (To Cádiz), dated 1831, is a patriotic cry against the oppressor, probably Napoleon. "Era un sueño" (It Was a Dream) casts a reminiscent backward glance upon dreams and hopes of the poet's youth, now lost. "La fuente" (The Fountain) briefly describes a fountain, surrounded by flowers; its laughing discourse is like the clear morning. "El centinela" (The Sentry) depicts a sentry thinking, sadly, of his childhood, his distant Andalucía, and of when he said farewell to his mother; she should not weep if he dies in battle.

Early morning returns him to the reality of the proximity of the enemy, and battle commences. "A Delisa" is a love plaint; Delisa should not know he suffers for her, since she will only laugh. "A.C.M." also evokes the lost dreams of the poet; he regrets being so cold and curses the things that make other people happy, but the love of a woman revives him. Flowers of the soul, come back and gladden my heart, he begs.

"A los defensores de Bilbao" (To the Defenders of Bilbao) begins with an opposite note to that of "A Cádiz"; this time the poet sings the bravery of the men who saved Spain. "Traducción de Victor Hugo" (A Victor Hugo Translation) is a description of love's awakening a young girl. The language seems less a translation than an interpretation in the poet's own words, a variation on the idea of Hugo. "Para el album de una señorita" (For the Album of a Young Lady) seems almost a commissioned description of the enchanting lady, but the meter changes and the poet makes allusions to her thorns and indifference. At the end he wished she would have thorns for everyone except for him. In "La noche de verano" (A Summer Night) silence and darkness are most welcome by the poet, who now can cry, concealed, and sigh unashamedly; the breeze may take his thoughts to his lady love. "Respeto" (Respect) is a warning to a girl that her eyes may reveal her feelings, and someone might take advantage of them.

In "Ambición" (Ambition) the poet asks that this passion take hold of those who thrive on it, but not of him, as he only desires not to covet anything. "La dádiva del poeta" (The Gift of the Poet) declares he is poor, but his heart and his art will adorn his beloved's brow. "El sueño" (Sleep) is another love poem in which the artist invokes sleep as a means to bury in darkness and silence his anguish; let the night take his plaint to his beloved. "En un album" (In an Album) seems to be a short piece written in an album upon request; if the heart is an altar, come into mine, he says, so I will adore you. "La vida" (Life) is another translation from Victor Hugo. This time his love is fulfilled, since his shepherdess shares his life. In "Profecía de Nahún" (The Prophecy of Nahun), with a certain biblical flavor, the poet expounds the prophecy of the imminent destruction of Nineveh, immersed in sin. The first three stanzas, warning of the troubles ahead, are repeated at the end. "La primera edad" (Adolescence) affirms that the poet knows that the early years are filled with laughter and dreams of pure love; he wasted his youth that way. He tells a young girl she should enjoy that stage of life, but before those dreams turn to tears it would be better for her to lose her life. "La garza" (The Heron) presents a majestic heron in flight as the poet warns it of the dangers of storms; his own flight was also toward a bright sun, but clouds darkened it and he lost his wings and his hope. "La despedida del cruzado" (The Farewell of the Crusader) employs a beautiful, pathetic contrast: a beautiful morning greets the sad moment of his parting; he leaves peace and love to go to war; his beloved should not hold back her tears, since they are a balm to him.

The last piece in this section is an excerpt from a lyric poem entitled "El sacristán de Toledo" (The Sexton of Toledo). At the end, García Gutiérrez notes this work was set for performance in the Cruz Theater during the theatrical season of 1839–40. The conditions and demands made by the composer (unidentified) forced the dramatist to alter the piece so much that only part of what he transcribes in the book was left. The dramatic potential is evident in this piece, wherein Hernando, a young man, loves a woman he sees at a distance from the belfry; a priests's choir is heard in the background. That night he is caught by surprise by a coven of witches flying on their brooms who come to rest in the belfry. One of the witches he recognizes as his lady love; he promises her his soul if she makes possible his wishes to fulfill an impossible love. Luzbel arrives, and they seal their pact. In the next scene Blanca is about to marry Don Diego, obviously against her will. A storm brews and Luzbel and Hernando appear. Blanca, Hernando's love, sees a way out, and since they love each other the wedding is called off, not without a great deal of commotion on the part of Don Diego and guests, but the power of hell is with Blanca and Hernando, so they will always be together. There is a sharp contrast between the prayers of the priests, the unrest Hernando feels, the thoughts of Blanca not wishing to become a powerful man's wife, and resorting to witchcraft to free herself. The triumph of hell is accorded a few choruses here.

III *Imitations of Seventeenth- and Eighteenth-Century Spanish Poets*

This section comprises twelve compositions. "Tristeza" (Sadness) asks a girl not to try to win the poet's love; he was hurt by Elisa's death and prefers silence to the easy promise love gives and then cuts short. "El ruiseñor" (The Nightingale) pursues the thought in asking the songbird not to break the night's silence; his melodies bring painful nostalgia. "La mariposa" (The Butterfly) is an invitation to the beautiful insect to take flight in search of honey to his beloved's lips; but be careful with her eyes, because they may burn its wings. "A una ingrata" (To an Ungrateful Woman) is a complaint; the poet would like to forget her and her treason, but he will always welcome her back. "La noche" (Night) is a long ode to the beauty of night, soothing everything, aided by the soft wind and majestic moonlight. "Abandono" (Abandon) is another lament of lost love, while in "La calma" (Calm) the poet states that, not being rich or ambitious, he has no fear of death. "A la aurora" (To Daybreak) welcomes the beautiful spectacle of dawn. "El primer amor" (First Love) is subtitled "letrilla" (a type of round in music which begins and ends the poem and also repeats two lines at the end of each stanza). An innocent girl knows the feeling of love, and the unrest it brings. "A la muerte de E . . ." (To E . . .'s Death) is another plaint inspired by the death of Elisa, while in "Soledad" (Solitude) the poet, wise and disillusioned, fears the storm he once admired and challenged, but Laura has gone away. Written in grandiloquent style, this long poem bemoans her absence, certain she will not return; his tears should not leave him, since he has nothing else left.

"Fingal," the last and longest of the poems, is a fantasy in five acts set in Celtic times. Bosmina bemoans the death of her mother, Monia, beside her grave; Sorglan tries to console her: Fingal left for war, but soon he will return. Rino, king of Caledonia, returns from war to find Monia dead. Their daughter, Bosmina, does not know he is her father. In act two, the girl again visits her mother's grave and rejects the love of Dutcaron. Fingal returns, and we learn that he and Bosmina are in love, but Rino, his father, keeps them apart without giving the reason although, according to him, all sorts of bad things will happen to the young lovers. Fingal cannot swear he will renounce Bosmina unless he knows why he is asked to do so; he is outraged when Rino is pleased with Dutcaron's wish to be given Bosmina as a wife. When Fingal suspects she is his sister, the only solution is for them to leave together, but the spirit of Monia and another unidentified ghost haunt her. The altar we see and a somber procession indicate that Bosmina is about to wed

Dutcaron. Rino laments the sorrow his children cause him. Fingal kills Dutcaron, who threatened to rob him of Bosmina, while Rino keeps speaking of doom, the curse on Fingal, and crime. Ultimately Fingal kills himself.

Much of the play is dedicated to advising Fingal and Bosmina, separately, about the doom they court, but the explanation of their relationship is long in coming. What is their crime? This needless tragedy places too much emphasis on the incestuous love of Fingal and Bosmina, who are totally innocent, without one word of sorrow from Rino, except for having seduced Monia, who even in death drives her daughter to despair. García Gutiérrez seems to be more at ease when relying on his own inspiration and not trying to imitate a genre alien to him, as in this piece. Despite the use of models, however, the language in the other poems is luminous, specific, and harmonious, and García Gutiérrez proclaims his admiration for the poets he imitates.

IV Luz y tinieblas (*Light and Darkness*)

"Luz y tinieblas" is subtitled "sacred and secular poems." The first part contains historic ballads, beginning with "El último Abderramen" (The Last Abderramen),[1] which depicts the crumbling Moorish empire in Córdoba, the defeat of the last ruler of that dynasty undermined by other Moorish tribes, and then Christianity recovering its land. The series "El conde de Saldaña" (The Count of Saldaña) concerns the sad story of the love of Jimena, sister of King Alfonso el Casto of Asturias, and the Count of Saldaña, forced to separate from his beloved, imprisoned and blinded (a subject treated by several other dramatists and poets), told by García Gutiérrez in five ballads and a conclusion. "El maestre de Alcántara" (The Master of Alcántara) depicts a fierce massacre of knights of the religious and military order of Alcántara which occurred in 1434, as the result of a Moorish ambush. The few survivors felt dishonored not to have been killed as well. King Juan II observed three days of mourning when he received the sad news.

The fourth and last title is "Los siete condes de Lara" (The Seven Counts of Lara), who are more commonly known as "infantes," as Entrambasaguas observes. In Burgos, at the wedding of Doña Lambra and Don Ruy Velázquez, the latter's seven nephews take part in the festivities and games of dexterity and valor, in which they excel, incurring the displeasure of Alvar Sánchez, cousin of the bride. Later she stops at nothing to take revenge on the young men, and even sways her husband to help her. He sends his brother Gustios, the boys' father, into Moorish territory, with a letter for Almanzor in which he asks that the messenger be killed. The Moorish king, annoyed at such a low act of treason, imprisons Gustios instead. Ruy Velázquez, under the pretext of avenging his brother's death, ventures into Moorish territory with other knights and his nephews, who are ambushed and killed, and their heads taken to Córdoba. Gustios's distrust of his brother is fully justified when, from his cell, he perceives the horrible crime Ruy has committed in killing the seven knights. The treacherous act fills all Christian Spain with sorrow and anger. Gustios has been consoled by a Moorish woman who took pity on him, and she is pregnant when the gentleman is freed. Fearful of Almanzor, she confesses her pregnancy, and the Moor encourages her to care for a son who might avenge the tragic treason. Years later the half-breed Mudarra, son of Gustios and the Moorish woman, wrought justice on Lambra and Ruy Velázaquez. The language is more evocative than poetic; that is, the images are strong, somber, and full of life even if that life is soon to be extinguished or will bring evil. The dramatic vein of García Gutiérrez predominates at all times.

V *The Second Part of* Luz y tinieblas

Headed "various poems," this section contains six pieces on religious subjects: "La muerte de Jesús" (The Death of Jesus), "Lamento del profeta Jeremías" (Lament of the Prophet Jeremiah), "Arrepentimiento" (Repentance), "Fragmento" (Fragment), "A la Virgen María" (To the Virgin Mary), and "Oración del profeta Jeremías" (Prayer of the Prophet Jeremiah). The titles are self-explanatory except for "Fragment," which compares the dark night, dawn, and all creation to an immense altar where man finds darkness and light. Without any separation other poems follow: "El lirio azul" (The Blue Lily), sad and ignored while the rose is acclaimed; "Recuerdos" (Memories), another yearning for lost dreams, the pain of love, and dead Elisa—the poet has no hope or aim; in his loneliness he wishes for death. "La luna" (The Moon) is a chant to the beauty and beacon light of the moon. "El invierno" (Winter) describes for

Elisa that season of the year. "Zulima," another Moorish ballad, follows: the brave Almanzor, three times victorious in battle, returns to Granada saddened because Zulima has betrayed his love. Her father is having her marry another. Almanzor, hidden, witnesses the start of the ceremony, and impulsively beheads the bridegroom. "A la reina Isabel II" (To Queen Isabel II) is dedicated to the young queen, whose mandate will be aided by all of Spain. "A Isabel II" (To Isabel II), in the same vein, uses a different meter. "Dudas" (Doubts) depicts the gloomy and tormented state of a man who moves in the dark toward an uncertain world where his soul will linger.

"Elvira"[2] is a tale in two parts, the first containing seven and the second six subdivisions, which begins with a reminiscence of childhood and carefree days. Elvira, a happy child, is beautiful and loved by all, but adolescence makes her feel the unrest of growing up. Her mother dies; she mourns her but soon falls in love with Pero Ansúrez Guzmán, a gentleman from León, who is wounded and made prisoner in Sevilla. Freed after a time, he conquers Elvira, like him a Christian living under Moorish domination. She is totally dedicated to making Pero Ansúrez happy, but when seen by King Abenhamet as he parades with his courtiers through the streets of Sevilla, she has a premonition of impending doom, and becomes sad. One night she is abducted and Ansúrez is left in a pool of blood. In part two Elvira, in the harem of the king, is expecting a child. One day she recognizes her lover in the eyes of a slave; Pero did not die. They communicate only through their eyes. Elvira shudders to think what will happen when the truth is known as the child is born. Meanwhile she suffers the sultan's love, hoping to be free some day. Abraham, a Hebrew doctor, detects her worry and elicits her secret, agreeing to have Ansúrez come to visit her. Both men, disguised, enter the palace without trouble, but the Jew had made a deal with the sultan, and when Elvira and her lover embrace they are caught. Pero kills his betrayer. The king and his men are ready to kill him, but Abenhamet recognizes Pero Ansúrez and orders that instead Elvira be thrown into the river. Pero's life is spared on the condition that he free the sultan's brother, imprisoned in León. Finally, "Al rey de España Amadeo I" (To Amadeo I, King of Spain) is an ode to the new king brought to Spain in the absence of an heir to the throne; therefore it has a somewhat historical tone.

VI *"Poesías Sueltas" (Unrelated Poems)*

This unnumbered section contains exactly what the title indicates. The first is "El duende de Valladolid, tradición yucateca" (The Ghost of Valladolid, a Yucatecan Tradition). Entrambasaguas summarizes it in part as found in the *Informe Contra Idolorum del Obispado de Yucatán* (A Report against Superstition of the Yucatán Diocese), written in Latin and Spanish by Don Pedro Sánchez de Aguilar, a priest, on the occasion of being summoned in 1596 to conjure and drive away the mishchievous ghost.

This ghost appeared in Valladolid, Yucatán (Mexico), in 1560, and would talk to people in the dark, so nobody ever saw him at all. His visits were quite frequent, especially to two houses, with whose dwellers he held conversations; in other houses he would make loud noises, so everyone was aware of his existence. At times the people most visited would ask him to play the guitar, which he did very well. The local priest decided to try to get rid of the ghost, and to that effect he went, disguised, and with the necessary items for the ritual, including a hyssop, to the two houses most frequented, but the ghost did not answer his call. However, upon returning home, the priest found mule excrement in the platter where he had left food for his supper, and the wine container was filled with a related suspicious liquid. Then the bishop decided to put an end to the pranks and decreed stiff penalties for those who disobeyed the order to ignore the ghost. Not being spoken to, and receiving no answers, the ghost cried aloud, the noises increased in some houses, and he even set some on fire. This brought a full-scale effort to exorcise the ghost and people responded, but at the last minute they left the priest alone in the procession. With the intervention of St. Clement, Pope and martyr, whose portrait with a bound demon at his feet is in the main altar of the church, the ghost was silenced for more than thirty years, but returned in 1596, setting afire houses in nearby Indian villages, for which reason the priest was summoned to remedy the situation. Entrambasaguas quotes only that far.

Harvey L. Johnson (number IX, pp. 158–60 of *Nueva Revista de Filología Hispánica,* 1955) adds a few bits of information to Entrambasaguas's notes, used as a starting point in the edition of García Gutiérrez's poetry. Written in Spanish, the Johnson article contains a description of the codex where the original version was consigned, and the affirmation that Justo Sierra O'Reilly made it available to

García Gutiérrez during his stay in Mérida. García Gutiérrez's subsequent treatment caused the legend to be printed again, enjoying a sort of revival. He incorporates into the tale the opposition Francisco de Vargas and Juana Guzmán find to their love, since her father wants her to marry Osorio. The mischief of the ghost ends, coincidentally, when Pedro Guzmán agrees to admit Vargas as his son-in-law. García Gutiérrez has poured into his story a great deal of humor and local color, with the mention and description of Mexican utensils and instruments. His pen flows easily, as if in haste to get to the end, in the hope of finding a new source of gaiety as he completes each step of the story.

"La cita a la madrugada" (Date at Dawn) states that the poet loves Juana, and would give his blood for her, but he is also human, so she should let him sleep in the morning. In another vein, in "Al Cardenal Cisneros" (To Cardinal Cisneros), the poet says: if you could return, you would be so happy to see the triumph of the lion of Spain over the tiger of Africa. "Carta a Filena" (A Letter to Filena) is an imitation of a Scottish poem: Filena kissed the poet, and he has not been able since to think of anything else. "El hipócrita" (The Hypocrite) presents one seemingly humble, whose god is money; he looks at the ground as he walks because his conscience is so heavy he cannot lift his head. "Amor sin celos" (Love without Jealousy) states that as the constant green of the fields and blue of the skies, and the sunlight without night would tire him, her eyes made him fall in love, but their total clarity and light made her eyes cold, so his love died. "Fragmento" (Fragment) relates the progression of the anxiety of taking a wife, from the romantic feelings experienced to the mother-in-law inspection, the expenses of the wedding, and then . . . hell. "Cantata a Calderón" is in four parts, two recited, each followed by a chorus, in praise of Calderón de la Barca, alive in our hearts. "El sepulcro de Evarina" (Evarina's Grave) is an imitation of Ossian. Beautiful Evarina died young and without having experienced love. "El día 2 de Mayo de 1808" (May 2, 1808) offers a sad, patriotic lament of the invasion of Spain by the French.

"La serenata" (Serenade) exhorts a girl not to hide her beauty in her house; or does she not know what love is? "A una valenciana en un baile de máscaras" (To a Valencian Girl at a Masked Ball) suggests that the poet would like to see her face, but if she is going to resent him he would prefer to look at her in wonder. "Desaliento"

(Dismay) presents another plaint for lost childhood, dreams of a wonderful world, hope, and glory not to be attained. The thoughts of the child are withered, and saying farewell to the dream of glory, the poet prepares to rest, having lost his strength. "Abajo los Borbones" (Down with the Bourbons) exalts the end of a tyranny, not really knowing what lies ahead; the poem appears rather to have been composed on the spur of the moment, in the heat of the occasion. The first part is to be recited; the other two, identical in meter, could be those for which Emilio Arrieta composed music, but this point is not made clear in the text. Entrambasaguas opines that García Gutiérrez displayed very poor judgment in writing this hymn against the Bourbon royal family when Isabel II was dethroned in 1868. In "La tumba ignorada" (The Forgotten Tomb), the poet searches in vain for the tomb of a loved one who, innocent, and a victim of others, was unhappy in life and death; she is a lost treasure. "A Don Adelardo López de Ayala" (To Adelardo López de Ayala) offers a tribute to this distinguished orator and writer. The manuscript of an unpublished poem titled "A la Sra. Da. A. J." (To Mrs. A. J.) is a veiled complaint over lost love, presumably hers. Entrambasaguas adds an appendix that lacks an explanation of what it is, variations or errata. An index of first verses and of titles closes the book.

In general, the poetry of García Gutiérrez is clear, with precise images, whether conveyed through one stanza or ten. He seems to know exactly when to stop description, as if using a living model, and describes appearance, mood, thoughts, feelings, the moment at which he sees the person or his surroundings, and what the action is or is going to be. Once the poet has made a point he goes on to the next, leaving a sense of freshness, be it beautiful or the imminence of a terrible happening, but always as if he were present. The reader feels this and, with the subtle pull and flow of the verses, is transported to the scene by the poet, aware of his emotional state at the moment of creation.

CHAPTER 10

Conclusion

AS already observed in part IV of chapter 2, dealing with *El trovador* and its unparalleled success, critics of all periods praise García Gutiérrez for many reasons, and seem unable to find fault amid such beauty, lyricism, emotional impact, and dramatic artistry. The first performed play of García Gutiérrez therefore overshadows his entire production, although other plays such as *Simón Bocanegra* and *Venganza catalana* enjoyed considerable public acclaim. Exceptions to the total surrender to our author's emotional appeal are Marcelino Menéndez y Pelayo and, to some extent, those critics who focus on written literature, confusing theater with it, such as, at times, Nicholson Adams and Lomba y Pedraja. This appeal to feelings is also suggested very strongly by some of García Gutiérrez's poetry, especially in long poems such as "Las dos rivales" (The Two Rivals), "El conde de Saldaña" (Count Saldaña), and "Los siete condes de Lara" (The Seven Counts of Lara). The imagery evokes living persons entangled in their problems against a background suggestive of a dramatic production more than an account of the tragedy of their lives.

For one with such an easy pen, capable of writing in verse as if no other form existed, García Gutiérrez is clearly more inclined to do justice to any subject in dramatic form. Hence his greater popularity as a dramatist than as a poet. This quality also explains why, at times, his characters reach heights inaccessible to actors, as pointed out by López Funes in the case of Ramiro, the monk king, although not the only one if we pay attention to García Gutiérrez's many creations. I regret having to eliminate from this book, because of space limitations, many direct quotations; detailed plot résumés (especially of *zarzuelas*); bringing out the implied or explicit humor in many scenes, and, especially, the staging of many of García Gutiérrez's plays. Powerful in dramatic situations, subtle and refreshing in his humor, foolproof in his plot intrigues, his works have universal appeal. Our author, in his plots, seems to have been fascinated by or drawn to impossible loves. It is most often the woman whose feelings are a source of torture, who is unable to control her emotions except on the surface, while burning desperately in a joyless world. García Gutiérrez does nothing to soothe her suffering; rather, he adds to her misfortune or inflicts more pain, making her helplessness in her torturous plight complete. This lack of solution points to a firsthand knowledge of a similar state; if we are to believe that an author reflects part of himself in most of his writings, this particular aspect is quite patent in García Gutiérrez, who may have disguised a particularly agonizing personal experience by channeling it through his feminine dramatic creations. Be that as it may, their anguish is quite real.

After reading many of his plays, one necessarily concludes that García Gutiérrez was also much attracted to historic figures and episodes. In the case of the latter, he seems to have been concerned with the lot of the poor in the sense of being a member of the working class, no matter how well remunerated, as opposed to the nobility; in a way, he denounces a collective type of injustice coming from those who are not aware of the plight of the downtrodden or of the right of the humble to defend their dignity and livelihood without being exploited. Sometimes their attitude resulted from unawareness of how the less fortunate people lived; in other instances it was due to personal traits that made them purposely blind to such things. Not wishing to experience the life of the less fortunate, a shield was always between them, protecting thereby a continuing rule devoid of human understanding. Another aspect of García Gutiérrez's work is the theme of injustice or ungratefulness, exemplified by various characters depicted by our author, some literally historic, others open to interpretation as to whether they actually behaved that way, or the intrigue was modified to highlight another aspect of the historic figure. What they have in common is biting the hand that brought them joy, love, freedom, or a kindness of some type.

Some are unfortunate because of their elders, who dealt them a blow or made them pay for their sins, as if the innocent had the obligation to cleanse their ancestor's stains. This type of plot is too abundant in García Gutiérrez's production not to suggest a reflection of the experience of the author at some point in his life. The instances of unfulfilled love, or of destiny bringing misfortune to those who obviously are not in a position to guide their life, point to his own youthful sensations. Some difficult choices made by his characters reflecting or resulting in either another's unhappiness, or the protagonist's, reveal frustrations or hard decisions made by a mature person. From his early writings there is a melancholy, a sensibility, and a somewhat pessimistic outlook that dominate other aspects of his writings, a quality that makes the reader forget or ignore occasional anachronisms, because the conflict is so powerful.

García Gutiérrez is not devoid of humor, a vein he allowed to surface occasionally: *El caballero de industria* (The Cunning Gentleman), *La espada de Bernardo* (Bernard's Sword), *El robo de las sabinas* (The Rape of the Sabines), *El capitán negrero* (The Slave-dealer Captain), "Un baile en casa de Abrantes" (A Dance in Abrantes's House), "El duende de Valladolid" (The Ghost of Valladolid), and many scenes from other plays attest to it. The great sense of artistry he possessed shows unequivocally in many of his plays, especially when he succinctly indicates what the stage should look like. In few words, García Gutiérrez can bring to the mind's eye a complicated scene from the standpoint of the stage director or the person in charge of costumes and properties. The mixture is such that it is difficult to discern whether a period of happiness triggered the writing of humorous or happy episodes, or if it was the product of a fortunate time when he could rid his mind and heart of sad and painful interludes, to write in a more serene frame of mind.

A truly artistic soul, then, is what Antonio García Gutiérrez possessed, which accounts also for the unevenness of his plays; some were more forceful than others and met with more success, while still others were deemed mediocre. This aspect of García Gutiérrez's writing has been called by some critics (among them his contemporary Antonio Ferrer del Río) laziness or indifference. It may have seemed so, but García Gutiérrez could hardly broadcast his inner state of mind or feelings so as to counteract the hasty judgments of others, likewise subject to fluctuation; they, not being in the public eye, as was our dramatist, could vent their feelings in a different way. García Gutiérrez, like any other author, must be evaluated taking into consideration trends that emerge after reading their works or in some other way experiencing their artistry. Lyricism, emotion, and sensibility are the core of the artistry of García Gutiérrez.

It would be unfair to convey the impression that everything is mildness and beauty in García Gutiérrez. There are some powerful scenes in his plays, tragic events and cruelty, depicted or staged, if the text is followed accurately, that appeal to emotions difficult to control. The element that makes them seem less unsavory than in plays by other authors is the precise touch García Gutiérrez gives them: they are suggested, recited, or given a moment on stage with the exact amount of time, a precise timing neither detracting from their tremendous impact on the audience, nor dwelling on them. Incidents such as the description of the bell of Huesca, the death of Manrique, the misfortunes of the page, or Simón Bocanegra's finding his beloved in a casket are all elements that belong to the drama, and the author left them there. Injustice and cruelty exist in the world, and there are many victims. García Gutiérrez makes their lot known with all the precision and feeling of the great artist he is. The sting is most certainly felt, but one is left under the impression that it came not from a bee, but from a butterfly. This is the García Gutiérrez that appealed to Verdi, striking a similar chord in his sensitivity, so the words and the music in a given situation tear apart the most hardened person in the audience.

Notes and References

Chapter One

1. In the *Espasa Calpe* encyclopedia (first edition, 1924), a note states that Leandro Fernández de Moratín was the first to receive such an honor in Spanish theaters in 1814, after the initial performance of his play *The Baron*. Joaquín de Entrambasaguas quotes Fernando Díaz-Plaja as observing that the practice existed in France since 1793, but neither mentions Moratín.

2. There is a reference to a similar coronation following a performance of *Simón Bocanegra*.

3. *Biografía de hombres célebres*. Oficina del Establecimiento Central. Madrid, 1843.

4. "1811. 10 Mars. Mme. Hugo va rejoindre, avec ses enfants, son mari, promu général depuis le 20 Aôut 1809. Trois mois de voyage pour rejoindre Madrid.... Sur les routes d'Espagne, il est frappé par la tragique beauté des sites et des villes: Ernani, Torquemada, Tolosa, Burgos, Valladolid, l'Escurial. Du collège des Nobles, a Madrid, il conserve le souvenir d'un nain difforme, tenent lieu de valet, que apparaîtra maintes fois dans son oeuvre, ainsi que le nom d'un de ses camarades espagnols, Elespuru, que deviendra celui d'un des fous de *Cromwell*." Victor Hugo, *Téatre Complete*, I. Bibliotèque de Pléiade. Préface by Roland Purnal. Notices et notes par J.J. Thierry et Josette Mélèze (Monaco, 1963), chronologie, p. xxi.

5. I had no access to the microfilm of *part of* this book until after my study was completed; therefore, judgments made by me were reached before finding agreement or added information in López Funes. Unfortunately the only copy of this book I found accessible stops at page 143, due to piracy from an irresponsible person who cut the rest; therefore my conclusions and opinions that coincide with López Funes have to be taken at face value since I had hunted for this study, in vain, for a long time. I find what portion of it exists of much value.

6. According to Harvey L. Johnson there is also a translation from the French play *Le demoin de la nuit* (The Night Devil) by Jean François,

Alfred Bayard, and Etienne Aragon not cited in any bibliography of García Gutiérrez, and published for the first time by Professor Johnson.

7. On page 305 of his *Galería de la literatura*, 1846, Antonio Ferrer del Río mentions a law that prohibits writers and booksellers from appropriating anybody's work until fifty years after their death, provided the heirs have not reedited them within the last ten years.

Chapter Two

1. In Teatro Español Borrás, volume 103, in the last page of *El rey monge*, 1837, the plays and writings (in thirteen volumes) of Fígaro, penname of Mariano José de Larra, are advertised. A similar though less exhaustive note is found at the end of *Margarita de Borgoña*, 1836. This points to the importance of Larra as a critic, public figure, and writer in general, as well as to the impact of his suicide at the age of twenty-seven.

2. Not always, as proven by the very stubborn Don Ferriz of *El rey monge* and other fathers, and the very strong women such as María in *El Encubierto de Valencia*, Elvira in *El caballero leal*, and Clemencia in *El premio del vencedor*; also many in secondary roles such as Braulia in *Magdalena*, Leonor in *Los desposorios de Inés*, Inés in *De un apuro otro mayor*, Elena in *Gabriel*, and many others before and after 1846, when Ferrer del Río writes.

3. See in the text my comments on Lomba y Pedraja in this section. The point is more fully explained in my book on Juan Eugenio Hartzenbusch published in the TWAS series, number 501.

Chapter Three

1. Braulia: "Yo que me muero por un palmo del Prado, y por una delantera de cazuela en el teatro del Príncipe, no de la Cruz, que no llega hasta ese punto mi afición, y verme aquí obligada a estar metida en casa sin una pulgada de paseo, ni una mala comedia romántica."

2. Samuel. A footnote at this point informs the reader that such a passage was discovered in 1248, and runs under a good portion of Sevilla.

Chapter Four

1. Mossén Frederic Moscardó Cervera, *Breu compendi de la història de Valencia*. V. Cortell (Valencia, 1953), p. 186.

2. This passage of *El caballero leal* refers back to the action of the García Gutiérrez play *El bastardo*, already discussed in this section, wherein King García is yet a prince.

3. This episode is the theme of *Elvira*, a tale in two parts, found in *Luz y tinieblas*, chapter 9, section V.

4. The *Espasa Calpe* encyclopedia also notes this episode (volume XXV, pp. 801–803).

5. Simón Bocanegra had a brother, Gil, a sailor, who from 1340 was in the service of King Alfonso XI. Founder of the Bocanegra Spanish branch, Gil died in 1372.

6. Hartzenbusch states that *De un apuro otro mayor* was written by García Gutiérrez in cooperation with two other writers, but the edition consulted, volume 203 of *Teatro*, mentions only our author.

7. "Anda, en su cuarto."

8. It is not clear in the case of *Gabriel* who is who at the beginning, a way to keep the intrigue going, and one wonders if Elena loves Juan why they have such a calculated and cold conversation about Jaime and Inés.

9. Curra says "Yo tuve maire también . . . ," and Manuel rejoins, "Yo de eso me regosijo, aunque osté nunca me dijo. . . ."

10. Inés has taken "Tres onsas de cardeniyo."

11. Manuel says, "Inés, sin adulasión, jas hecho una tontería."

Chapter Five

1. This scene of *Los milonarios* depicts the low-class quarters of Madrid with a great deal of color in the names, language and characters.

2. "Examinado este drama, creo que debe prohibirse por su tendencia política, y creo que debe prohibirse tanto mas, cuanto el drama es bueno. —Madrid, 26 de Octubre de 1865.—El Censor de Teatros.—Narciso Serra."

Chapter Six

1. This seems to reflect the concept some people had of the music of Verdi, a contemporary composer. Esteban says, "Sí, en fin, repasa tu repertorio clásico." Cecilia: "Nada de Verdi?" Esteban: "¿De Verdi? ¡Ni por asomo! Es muy delicado, y esa es musica para sordos."

Chapter Seven

1. This is the most popular *zarzuela* of García Gutizérrez, and it has a sequel; for this reason more detail is given concerning the plot.

Chapter Eight

1. *Histoire illustrée de la litérature française*, par Emil Abry, Charles Audic, et Paul Crouzet (Paris, Didier 1946), p. 64: "D'Après une anecdote, sans doute controuvée, Molière aurait déclaré que sans le *Menteur* il

n'aurait peut-être jamais fait le *Misanthrope*. La vérité est que Molière a empruntée d'autres de ses prèdecesseurs beaucoup plus qu'à Corneille."

2. Huszar also observes that *Le roi s'amuse* is similar to Rojas's *García del Castañar*.

3. Steven Runciman defends Juan de Prócida, who appears as a great conspirator in "such dramatic versions of the story as the tragedies of *Les Vêpres Siciliennes*, by Casimir Delavigne, and the *Massacre at Palermo* by Mrs. Felicia Hemans and in the absurd libretto written by Scribe for Verdi's opera *Il Vespro Siciliano*." Runciman rather believes the historic accounts of Michele Amari, an Italian historian, and two other Catalans, who state the Aragonese merely took charge of the government of the island in turbulent times. Steve Runciman, *The Sicilian Vespers. A History of the Mediterranean World in the Later Thirteenth Century* (Cambridge, England, 1958), p. 288.

4. Servando: Todo, en fin,/ era gracia y melodía/ en que apenas se atrevía/ a propasarse el violín. . ./ Pero hoy, con ese rimbombo/ infernal y esa anarquía/ y tanta trompetería/ y tanto zurrar el bombo. . . ."

Chapter Nine

1. Commonly Abderramán, it reads in this text Abderramen.

2. This episode of Elvira is treated in García Gutiérrez's play *Zaida*, already discussed in chapter 4, part V.

Selected Bibliography

PRIMARY SOURCES

Poesías de Don Antonio García Gutiérrez. Madrid: Boix, 1840.
Luz y Tinieblas. Madrid: Boix, 1842.
Obras escogidas de Don Antonio García Gutiérrez. Madrid: Rivadeneyra, 1866.
Teatro Español and *Teatro Español Borrās*, collections in which most García Gutiérrez plays are found. For a list of works the reader is referred to chapter 1, part III, and to the index, under the author's name.

SECONDARY SOURCES

ADAMS, NICHOLSON BARNEY. *The Romantic Plays of García Gutiérrez*. New York: Instituto de las Españas en Estados Unidos, 1922. Although the study is rather complete in some cases, and the analysis of a given play may be revealing to the uninitiated, the book contains a number of misleading statements and some errors, particularly when trying to ascribe influences that do not exist or are contradictory.

ALICNA FRANCH, JUAN. *Teatro romántico*. Barcelona: Bruguera, 1968. Alcina has read what others have written about the same subject and added his own opinions. There are omissions and errors of various types, not all attributable to the printer. With increasing amounts of material to be read in order to make a study or prepare a book on dramatists, Alcina seems a bit careless.

ENTRAMBASGUAS, JOAQUIN de. *Poesías de Antonio García Gutiérrez*. Madrid: Aldus S. A. de Artes Gráficas, 1947. Contains the most complete collection of García Gutiérrez's poetry, with a long prologue which lacks clarity in some instances.

FERRER DEL RIO, ANTONIO. *Galería de la literatura*. Madrid: Mellado, 1846. García Gutiérrez is one of several figures portrayed by his contemporary Ferrer del Río, who also authorized a number of his plays to be performed.

GUAZA Y GOMEZ DE TALAVERA, CARLOS *Músicos, poetas y actores*. Madrid: Maroto e Hijos, 1884. Guaza makes a study of the life, artistic endeavors and contributions to the national roster of distinguished men of several musicians, old and contemporary, and some writers and actors. The information given on some is sporadic, and such is the case of García Gutiérrez.

LARRA, MARIANO JOSE DE. *Artículos de crítica literaria y artística*. Edición de José Lomba y Pedraja in Clásicos Castellanos, volume 52. Madrid: Espasa-Calpe, 1960. Among other items, this book contains the critique in two parts of *El trovador*.

LOPEZ FUNES, ENRIQUE. *Don Antonio García Gutiérrez, estudio crítico de sus obras dramáticas*. Madrid: Suárez, 1900; Cádiz: Alvarez, 1900. A most difficult book to find, the only copy extant in a United States library (Hispanic Society of America) is incomplete; worth studying for the García Gutiérrez plays it covers.

LOMBA Y PEDRAJA, JOSÉ. *García Gutiérrez, Venganza catalana* and *Juan Lorenzo*. Clásicos Castellanos, volume 65. Madrid: Espasa- Calpe, 1958. Contains a very informative prologue that falls short where he includes what others have said, sometimes without further checking. A good source of information due to the availability of the collection.

NOVO Y COLSON, PEDRO DE. *Autores dramáticos contemporáneos y joyas del teatro español del siglo XIX*. Madrid: Fortanet, 1881. With a prologue by Antonio Cánovas del Castillo, this book offers a valuable source of material relating to the Romantic period and information about writers of the time. The part written by Cayetano Rosell on García Gutiérrez provides biographical material, discusses his work and artistry, as well as the play included, *Juan Lorenzo*, and gives information about its censor, Narciso Serra. A list of García Gutiérrez's titles published since the Hartzenbusch catalogue in *Obras escogidas* is also provided.

1. Other Reference Material

Excluding histories of literature, dictionaries, encyclopedias, reference books known to every Hispanist, and many other books consulted whose contribution is negligible, or that deal with aspects of Romanticism in general or other authors inapplicable here, the following titles helped to clarify some aspects of this book.

BLANCO GARCIA, FRANCISCO. *La literatura española del siglo XIX*. Madrid: Aguado, 1891. Fr. Blanco, an Augustinian monk, attempted to compile an anthology improving upon those existing at the time. His judgment tends to have a moral and religious slant that sometimes overlooks the fact that he is dealing with theater.

BURGUERA SERRANO, R.P., FR. . AMADO DE CRISTO (O. F. M.) *Representaciones escénicas malas, peligrosas y honestas*. Barcelona: Librería

Católica Internacional, 1911; Valencia: López y Cía., 1915. In three volumes, this moral qualification of plays has an extensive prologue explaining the approach to such censorship, but presents facets of theater little studied.

ESPASA-CALPE, *Enciclopedia universal ilustrada.* Barcelona, 1924. A good source of supplementary information, even though not always reliable.

FLOREZ DE SETIEN, FR. ENRIQUE. *Memoria de las reinas católicas de España.* Madrid: Aguilar, 1945 (original edition, 1761), volume I. Volume II: Marín 1770. Good reference for checking queens and their relationship with their husbands and children, the book also includes women who bore royal children without being queens.

HUSZAR, GUILLAUME. *L'influence de l'Espagne sur le téatre français des XVIII et XIX siècles.* Etudes critiques de litérature comparée. Paris: Honoré Champion, 1912. An exceptional book in contents and the approach of the author, truly an essay in comparative literature taking into consideration national characteristics.

LOPEZ FUNES, ENRIQUE. *Don Alvaro o la fuerza del sino.* Estudio crítico. Cádiz: Alvarez, 1899. Being one of the major Romantic plays, its study is indispensable in evaluating the period, including the operatic version of some plays.

MARTIN, GEORGE. *Verdi, His Life and Times.* New York: Dodd, Mead, and Co., 1963. The very complete biographical data on Verdi provides as well much pertinent information as to his place in Romanticism, his tastes, and his being drawn to so many works by his contemporaries, especially Victor Hugo and the Spanish playwrights.

MESONERO ROMANOS, RAMON DE. *Memorias de un setentón.* Madrid: Renacimiento, 1926 (original edition, 1881). Among much data relating to Romantic times, the *Parnasillo* is included.

MOSCARDO CERVERA, MOSSEN FREDERIC. *Breau compendi de la història de València.* Valencia: Cortell, 1953. A priest, Fr. Moscardó compiled laboriously from many sources this history of the kingdom of Valencia, written in the vernacular (Valenciano).

SERIE KOEL. *Prontuario cronológico de historia de España.* Madrid: Pueyo, 1941. A good reference for historic dates and events.

WEAVER, WILLIAM. *Verdi Librettos in New English Translation with the Original in Italian.* Garden City, New York: Anchor Books, Doubleday and Company, 1963. More accurate than others in rendering a given text, his comments are constructive from the standpoint of the background operagoers often miss.

Index

(The works of Antonio García Gutiérrez are listed under his name.)

Adams, Nicholson B., 39–41, 47, 53, 75, 79, 91, 100, 102, 108, 121, 123, 125, 157
Alcina Franch, Juan, 40–42, 47, 75, 108
Alfonso I, the Warrior King, 50
Alfonso VI, King, 71, 72
Alfonso VII, King, 119
Angelo (Hugo), 21
Argote de Molina, Gonzalo, 40
Arrieta, Emilio, 23, 130, 132–37
Asenjo Barbieri, Francisco, 23, 130, 131, 135
Asquerino, Eduardo and Eusebio, 24
Aulestia i Pijoan, Antonio, 102

Barbieri, Francisco Asenjo, see Asenjo
Bardare, Leone Emanuele, 141
Bataglia di Legnano, La (Verdi), 144
Blanco Garcia, Fr. Francisco, 38, 43, 47, 53, 78, 79, 100, 108, 119
Bocanegra, Simón, 87
Bofarull, Antonio de, 102
Boito, Arrigo, 142
Boix, Ignacio, 27
Boldún, Elisa, 119
Borgoña, Ramón de, 119
Bourgeois, A., 25
Brett, Lewis E., 108
Burguera y Serrano, Fr. Amado de Cristo, 42, 43, 47, 51, 53, 72, 102, 108

Caballero, Manuel Fernández, see Fernández
Calabria, Duke of, 110
Calderón de la Barca, Pedro, 20, 21, 33, 38, 40, 131

Caltañazor, Vicente, 138
Calvet, Francisco, 138
Camí del sol, Lo (Guimerá), 102
Cammarano, 140, 141
Cancionero de Baena, 39, 40
Cárdenas, José de, 119
Catherine Howard (Dumas), 39
Cayron, Salvadora, 112
Cervantes, Miguel de, 21
Charles V, King (Carlos I of Spain), 86, 109
Collé, 133
Comuneros of Castile, 86
Conjuración de Venecia, La (Martínez de la Rosa) 19
Corneille, 20, 140
Covarrubias, 43
Cromwell (Hugo), 21, 139

Diez, Matilde, 97, 100, 119
Don Alvaro o la fuerza del sino (Saavedra), 19, 20, 22, 36, 38, 39, 139
Don Carlo (Verdi), 143
Don Carlos (Schiller) 143
Donizetti, Gaetano, 143
Duca d'Alba, Il (Donizetti), 144
Dumas, Alexander, 19, 20, 25, 38, 39, 47
Duque de Rivas, see Saavedra, Angel de

Enrique (rei encobert) 61, 110
Entrambasaguas, Joaquín de, 146, 147, 154, 156
era, Spanish or of Caesar, 66, 72
Ernani (Verdi), 143

Index

Fadrique de Aragón, King, 101
Fernández Caballero, Manuel, 23
Fernando el Católico, King, 110
Ferrer del Río, Antonio, 18, 36, 41, 60, 100, 103, 159
Flor, Roger de, 100, 101
Forza del destino, La (Verdi) 143
Francí, 110

García, Count of Castile, 80
Carcía, son of the king of Navarra, 69
García Gutiérrez, Antonio: biography, 15–18

WORKS-DRAMA:
Adaptations and translations, 24, 25
In cooperation with other writers, 24, 25
Obras escogidas (Selected Works) list, 25, 26
Original plays, 29–126
Bastard, The (El bastardo), 53–55, 69
Brave Woman, The (La mujer valerosa), 86, 126
Catalan Revenge (Venganza catalana), 16, 42, 69–86, 97–102, 108, 126, 134, 157
Children's story, A (Un cuento de niños) 27, 121–23, 144
Chrysalis and Butterfly (Crisálida y mariposa), 119–21
Cunning Gentleman, The (El caballero de industria), 27, 63–66, 95, 125, 126, 159
Dance in Abrantes's House, A (Un baile en casa de Abrantes), 145–47
Disguised Man of Valencia, The (El Encubierto de Valencia), 38, 58–61, 86, 110, 126
Doña Urraca de Castilla, 117–19, 125
Feelings of Hate and Love (Afectos de odio y amor), 92, 93
From trouble a Bigger one (De un apuro otro mayor), 81, 82
Gabriel, 82–84
Goodness Without Experience (La bondad sin la experiencia), 95
Grain of Sand, A (Un grano de arena), 27, 123–26
Juan Lorenzo, 42, 69, 86, 104–110, 126, 138
Loyal Gentleman, The (El caballero leal), 66–69, 72
Magdalena, 38, 51–53, 125
Millionaires, The (Los millonarios), 93–95, 126
Monk King, The (El rey monge), 38, 48–51, 79, 126
Nobility obliges (Nobleza obliga), 114–18, 126
Opposite Paths (Sendas opuestas), 112–14
Page Boy, The (El page), 38, 44–47, 126
Partial Eclipse (Eclipse parcial), 96–97
Pledges of a Revenge, The (Empeños de una venganza), 84–86
Prize of the winner, The (El premio del vencedor), 72–74
Reeds Turn Into Spears, The (Las cañas se vuelven lanzas), 102–104, 126
Samuel, 55–57
Secret of the Hung Man, The (El secreto del ahorcado), 87–89
Simon Bocanegra, 16, 40, 49, 75–79, 86, 126, 139, 157
Troubadour, The (El trovador), 15, 19, 20, 28–43, 50, 89–91, 125, 126, 139–41, 157
Uncle Tronera's Children (Los hijos del tío Tronera), 43, 89–91, 126
Wedding of Doña Sancha, The (Las bodas de Doña Sancha), 79
Wedding of Ines, The (Los desposorios de Inés), 61–63, 125
Zaida, 69–72, 125
WORKS-DRAMA-ZARZUELAS: 96, 128–38
Azon Visconti, 96, 130, 134
Bernard's Sword (La espada de Bernardo), 27, 96, 130, 131, 159
Call and Troop (Llamada y tropa), 27, 111, 130, 135

Night Suitor (Galán de noche), 111, 130, 136
One day of Reign (Un día de reinado), 130
Playboy or the Voluntary Lancer, The (El hijo de familia o el lancero voluntario), 130, 131
Rape of the Sabines, The (El robo de las sabinas), 96, 130, 134, 159
Return of the Pirate, The (La vuelta del corsario), 111, 130, 137
Royal Hunt, The (La cacería real), 96, 130, 133
Ship-boy, The (El grumete), 96, 130, 132, 137
Slave-dealer Captain, The (El capitán negrero), 111, 130, 137–38, 159
Tavern-keeper Girl of London, The (La tabernera de Londres), 111, 130, 137
To Become Blind in Order to See (Cegar para ver), 96, 130, 135
Two Crowns (Dos coronas), 130, 136
WORKS-POETRY: 23, 145–56
Imitarios of XVII and XVIII century Spanish poets, 149–51
Luz y tinieblas, I, 23, 151–52
Luz y tinieblas, II, 24, 152–53
Other poems, 153–56

Germana, Queen, 109, 110
germanía wars, 108, 109
Gil, Isidoro, 24, 25, 47
Gil de Zárate, Antonio, 16, 24
Gitanilla, La (Cervantes), 21, 39
González de Mendoza, Pedro (Cardinal), 61
González Mate, Pedro, 51
Guaza, Carlos, 37, 38, 41, 60, 66
Guimerá, Angel, 102
Guzmán, Antonio, 15, 33

Hartzenbusch, Eugenio Maximino, 42, 119
Hartzenbusch, Juan Eugenio, 20, 36, 41, 43
Hernani, (Hugo), 19, 21, 139
Hugo, Victor, 19–22, 38, 39, 139, 143, 148

Hurtado, Antonio, 114
Hurtado de Mendoza, Diego (Cardinal), 61, 110
Huszar, Guillaume, 20, 21, 140

Inés de Poitiers, 50
Inzenga, José, 136
I vespri siciliani (Verdi), 143
Il Duca d'Alba (Donizetti), 143

Jimena (concubine of King Alfonso VI), 72
Johnson, Harvey L., 154
Juan, Prince, 61

Karina, wife of Roger de Flor, 101

Lalama, Vicente, 27
Lamadrid, Bárbara, 80
Larra, Mariano José de, 20, 33–35, 37, 39, 40
Laurencin, 25
Lemoine, Gustave, 25
Lesage, 20
Lessing, 25
Lista, Alberto, 146
Lloréns, Juan, see Lorenzo
Lomba y Pedraja, José, 40, 42, 72, 97, 100, 102, 108, 114, 157
Lope de Vega, see Vega Carpio, Lope Félix de
López Funes, Enrique, 21, 22, 38, 47, 50, 51, 55, 57, 63, 66, 69, 72, 78, 126, 157
Lorenzo, Juan, 107, 108, 110
Lucrèce Borgia (Hugo) 21

Macías and Macías (Larra), 39, 40
Mañon (Hugo) 21
Manrique de Lara, Enrique (rei encobert), 61, 110
Marcelo, 117–19
Marchetti, 143
Marguerite de Borgogne (Dumas), 39, 47
Marguerite of Flanders, 61
Marie Tudor (Hugo), 39
Marion de Lorme (Hugo), 21
Marquis of Cenete, 61
Martin, George, 141, 143

Index

Martin El Empecinado, Juan, 140
Martínez de la Rosa, Francisco, 19, 20
medals, 16
Médico de su honra, El (Calderón), 21
Mellesville, 25
Menéndez y Pelayo, Marcelino, 51, 157
Menteur, Le (Corneille), 140
Misanthrope, Le (Molière), 140
Molière, 140
Moncada, Francisco de, 100
Moreno Carbonero, 102
Moro, Justo, 133
Muntaner, Ramón, 100

Navarro, Fernando, 17
Notre Dame de Paris (Hugo), 21, 39
Novo y Colson, Pedro de, 37, 41

Olona, D. L., 25, 133
Orientada, La (Ruiz), 102
Ossian, 155
Oudrid, Cristóbal, 132

Pacheco, María, 86, 87
Padilla, Juan, 86, 87
Palau y Dulcet, Antonio, 102, 132
Paleólogo, Andrónico, 101
Parnasillo, El, 20
Pérez Galdós, Benito, 22
Petronila, 50
Philip of Austria, Archduke, 61
Piave, Francesco Maía, 142
Piñero, Enrique, 100
Pitarra, S., 102
Porfiar hasta morir (Lope), 39
Porcel, 43
Príncipe, Augustín, 24

Quintana, Manuel José, 24

Ramiro II, the Monk King, 50, 69
Ramiro, son of King Sancho III, 55
Ramón Berenguer IV, Count, 50
Regensburguer, Carl August, 39, 40
Rennert, Hugo, 39
Rigoletto (verdi), 143
Rivas, Duke of, see Saavedra
Roger de Flor (García Gutiérrez), 16, 102

Roi s'amuse, Le (Hugo), 21, 143
Romanticism, 19
Rondor de Llobregat (Rubió), 102
Rosell, Cayetano, 18, 37, 41, 61
Rubió y Lluch, 102
Ruiz, 102
Ruiz, Salvador, 135
Ruiz de Alarcón, Juan, 140
Ruy Blas (Hugo), 143

Saavedra, Angel de, Duque de Rivas, 19, 20, 36, 39, 139
Sánchez de Aguilar, Pedro, Fr., 154
Sancho III of Navarra, King, 55, 69
Scribe, Augustin Eugène, 133, 137
Serra, Narciso, 109
Shakespeare, 33, 39
Sierra O'Reilly, Justo, 154
Simón Bocanegra (Verdi), 141–43
Soler, Federico, 102

Tejedor de Segovia, El (Ruiz de Alarcón), 40, 140
Tía fingida, La (Cervantes) 21
Torquemada (Hugo), 21
Tour de Neslé (Dumas), 47
Traviata, La (Verdi), 141
Trovatore, Il (Verdi), 43, 140–41, 143

Urgel, Count of, 43
Urraca of Castile, Queen, 119

Vega Carpio, Lope Félix de, 21, 38–40
Vela, Counts of, 80
Venganza de la Tana, La (Soler, Pitarra), 102
Verdad sospechosa, La (Ruiz de Alarcón), 140
Verdi, Giuseppe, 79, 139–41, 144, 160

Weaver, William, 141
Weil, Alexander, 21

Zaida, concubine of King Alfonso VI, 72
zarzuela (see also Works-Drama) 23, 26, 27, 96, 111, 128–38
Zorrilla, José, 24, 146
Zurita, Jerónimo, 43